D0975157

Rebuilding the House

Rebuilding the House

LAURIE GRAHAM

VIKING

VIKING
Published by the Penguin Group
Viking Penguin, a division of Penguin Books USA Inc.,
40 West 23rd Street, New York, New York 10010, U.S.A.
Penguin Books Ltd, 27 Wrights Lane, London W8 5TZ, England
Penguin Books Australia Ltd, Ringwood, Victoria, Australia
Penguin Books Canada Ltd, 2801 John Street, Markham, Ontario, Canada L3R 1B4
Penguin Books (N.Z.) Ltd, 182–190 Wairau Road, Auckland 10, New Zealand

Penguin Books Ltd, Registered Offices:
Harmondsworth, Middlesex, England

First published in 1990 by Viking Penguin,
a division of Penguin Books USA Inc.

1 3 5 7 9 10 8 6 4 2

Copyright © Laurie Graham, 1990
All rights reserved

Page 177 constitutes an extension of the copyright page.

LIBRARY OF CONGRESS CATALOGING IN PUBLICATION DATA
Graham, Laurie.
Rebuilding the house / Laurie Graham.
p.   cm.
I. Title.
ISBN 0–670–82891–2
PS3557.R2145R4   1990
813'.54—dc20   89–40667

Printed in the United States of America
Set in Garamond No. 3
Designed by Cheryl L. Cipriani

For George

Rebuilding the House

M y cat lies on her side, eyes wide, incredulous. The temperature is 95, the humidity is 95, and we have just moved to the country.

There is no air conditioning in this house. In fact, there isn't much of anything in this house. Built around 1900, it is a small, two-story farmhouse, architecturally undistinguished, but with a worn charm inside. The floors sag, but the floorboards are pine and of varying widths. The rooms are small but the ceilings are high. The doors and windows are narrow and tall. I know that the house is in poor condition. But I feel close to my husband here and I will stay here for a while.

I am limp with the heat. Or rather would be if I weren't so determined to unpack. My entire wardrobe hangs on rods in shoulder-high cartons in the kitchen. Fifty-plus cartons of books wait in the garage, along with a Chevy-Suburban-load of the miscellaneous stuff that at the last moment can't be

categorized as you pack your daily life into a box. Mariah scarcely raises her head as I stagger by with armloads of incongruously woolen clothes. Under my T-shirt my hand skims perspiration from my midriff as a squeegee skims water from a windshield. I have never been so hot. I assume Mariah's look of incredulity and it makes me laugh.

Mariah is fat, like a fireplug, and beautiful—tortoiseshell and white, with big round face and big, black-rimmed round eyes. She won my heart at Bide-A-Wee by burying her head in the crook of my arm as the attendants warned me against her viciousness. I could feel her yearning. Murray, her diametric opposite, is downstairs chewing up boxes. An orange and white tiger, tough, stocky, with hind legs like turkey thighs, he won me over that same day with his playfulness. He is endlessly entertaining, though I wonder sometimes, as he clatters by like a stampede of cossacks, whether I am strong enough to withstand such energy.

The house is so unprepossessing from the outside, asbestos shingles, once painted white, now worn to gray; window frames, once bright green, now cracked and faded. Tendrils of wisteria twist around porch posts. Hedges loom. Honeysuckle grows rampant over boxwood. The grass is at least shin high.

The porch runs along the front and one side of the house. Its concrete floor and railing of contoured block seem all the heavier for the slender wooden posts and for the rafters visible above. Weeds burst from behind the treads of the steps that lead off the front and off the side. More weeds push through the cracks in the concrete walk between the steps at the side and the driveway. Soil and grass have long since covered over the walk at the front. It is an entrance we never used.

Still, there are touches of a builder attempting to please. The cross gables on either side of the front-gabled roof. The green decorative arches over the small gable windows, echoing the arched upper panels of the double front doors. The bipartite transom over the doors.

We used the house only on occasional weekends. George had bought it, with its two-and-a-half-acre lot, in the sixties, for the land it was on, not to live in. Later, he built a garage at the back of the lot for his antique cars. It was only when the main house was sold that we spent any time in this one. It had been vacant for years.

Now, of course, it is the house that I lived in with my husband, the one place that belonged only to us. George was married and raised a family in the other house, and in the New York apartment. Although we lived in them together, those places were not mine. Much younger than he, I knew him only at the end of his life. Was his second wife.

Last January he died.

Vrooooom. Vrroooooooom. Vrrrrrooooooooooooooooooooo-ooooooom! The night is black as pitch. Hot. Another snorting, growling, grunting hulk rumbles through my bones. No one dreamed in 1900 of eighteen-wheelers, forty feet from the bedroom window. People out here ask me how anyone can sleep in New York, it's so noisy. Little do they know.

The house is situated in north-central New Jersey, in an area of green, rolling hills, fifty miles west of the Lincoln Tunnel. It is a world undreamt of by most New Yorkers, who know New Jersey only for the malodorous industrial complex that borders the New Jersey Turnpike between New York City and Newark airport. Known for its peaches, until the peach blight of 1900 to 1920 wiped out its peach-growing industry, the area remained unassuming farm country until recently, when an influx of corporations and the inexorability of suburban sprawl made development inevitable.

My house is the last of the mile-long row of houses and miscellaneous public buildings that line the county road after it crosses the old New Jersey Central, now the state-owned New Jersey Transit, railroad track. On the far side of that track is the group of buildings—post office, newsstand, drugstore, gasoline station, Union Hotel (Est. 1845)—that forms the nucleus of the town. The house stands on a slight rise, so that from certain vantage points its slender lines, its gabled roof appear to be lifting toward the sky.

The house is protected front and back by clusters of trees—maple, holly, cedar, tall long-needled pines. There is a flowering dogwood immediately outside the kitchen window and a rosebush grows in the shade of a Norway spruce. Everything is overgrown. The remainder of the lot is open, bordered on one side by shrubbery, on the other by a side road, and at the back by a stand of lilacs and the seven-car garage. Beyond the shrubbery, a small, single-story white frame house sits on its half-acre lot. Behind it, uncultivated fields undulate toward the gentle hills of the horizon. Across the side road, and facing more open fields, the newer developments begin.

"Are you all right out there?" people ask when I tell them I have moved to "the country." I think I am. It's an adventure to try a new kind of life after twenty years in New York. And I had no choice. After George died I couldn't afford the New York apartment. And New York is only fifty miles away. People worry that I won't be able to tolerate the change in my standard of living. They haven't stopped to consider that I still have what remains of the most wonderful thing in my life. And it is here.

I've never seen so many bugs. Centipedes, spiders, Japanese beetles, biting black ants, ticks, moths, endless others, wingèd and otherwise, that I can't identify. They drop out of trees. They crawl out of drains. They scuttle across my pillow at night. I search my body for the splotchy, spreading, central-clearing rashes of Lyme disease.

Earlier this evening I went briefly to the garage. An acquaintance, seeing the open door and the light, stopped to say hello. A few minutes later, as she prepared to leave, I flicked some sort of beetle from her windshield. I waved as she drove off, then turned to see hundreds of beetles, everywhere in the garage—marching over my stepson's 1936 Cadillac with clutching, sticklike legs; scuttling toward my boxes, big, fat, brown, thousands and thousands of beetles. I grabbed my can of House & Garden bug spray, guaranteed lethal to twenty-four specified varieties of crawling, flying, and garden bugs, and attacked them one by one, on the floor, in mid-flight as they soared toward the lights, on the car, in the aisles between my boxes. Bodies lay writhing, crashed from the air. Others fought back, dive-bombing into my hair, against my face. I ducked, beat them off, spraying, spraying. I had read the du Maurier story but could think only of Tippi Hedren in that phone booth in Alfred Hitchcock's film version of "The Birds."

Finally it was quiet. Beetles twisted or lay dead. Like an exhausted warrior, can in hand, I surveyed the carnage, the appalling sight of my garage littered with dead bodies. I turned out the lights, leaving the door open so that any remaining bugs would leave. Typical urbanite, I thought. That's all I had to do to begin with—turn out the lights. I felt embarrassed at the thought of all those bodies. I would have to sweep them up first thing tomorrow before anybody saw.

On the way back to the house, floating, sweeping, soaring, were the fireflies. There a flash, then over there, high, low, skimming the grass. I remember, as a child, cupping them in my hands to capture their glow.

I've always loved going for a ride. When we were young, in the era before television, my grandfather kept my brother and me entertained after dinner by taking us for a ride in his car. Each ride followed a route that had become sacrosanct in our minds and so unchanging, and we took turns choosing which ride we would take. My favorite was the one to the watering trough. (On exceptional occasions grandfather would take us to his farm to see the bull.)

I have two rides here already. One follows a narrow country road as it meanders alongside a stream, every mile or so passing a house or weathered barn nestled in a break in the trees. At the end of the ride is a small village green and the brave white façade of a country church. The other ride is through horse country—big white clapboard houses and big white clapboard stables, split-rail fences bordering acres of pasture. One is a cozy ride, the other a rich man's ride. But it is the quality of the light that astounds me, regardless of which ride I take on these summer evenings. Serene, yellow-gold, gracing the trees, grass, alternating with shadow. It is a light one simply doesn't see in the city and for me now it is a source of wonder.

The fertility of this place doesn't end with bugs. It is Wednesday, time to put out the garbage for the weekly pickup. I haul the brown Hefty bags out of my new plastic garbage can, and at the bottom of the can see fifteen or twenty short, squirming, cream-colored worms. What are they? Maggots?! Where did they come from? The garbage is wrapped in plastic. The can has a tight-fitting lid. Is this what they mean by "the environment"?!

The walls inside the house are painted white, and sheer white curtains hang at the windows. The curtains downstairs, embroidered with white floral panels, hang straight. The ones upstairs are plain, except for their classic ruffle, and tie back. White window shades are pulled halfway down behind them.

The furniture is nineteenth-century hodgepodge—my selection from the accumulation of our families over the years. It too is well worn, but seems to me to have a certain grace, especially the bed and the chair whose uprights culminate in an arcing curve to form the neck and the head of a swan.

In each downstairs room a steam pipe an inch and a half in diameter runs from floor to ceiling. The house was formerly heated by a coal furnace in the cellar. The heat rose to the first floor through a three-foot-square grate located at one end of the long, narrow room that we used as a dining room, and reached the second floor through a much smaller grate directly above. It wasn't until later that a modern oil furnace and radiators were installed. And of course it was easier and more economical to run the pipes through the rooms.

I am doing very little to the décor. George's collection of early automobile books still lines the walls of what the appraiser referred to as "the sewing room." A basket of hammers and screwdrivers and pliers sits on a cabinet near the door. I have added a framed color photograph of George driving his 1936 TT Replica Frazer Nash, an English racing car.

It is said that one must let go of one's grief, leave the

past behind and move on. A recent article in *The New York Times* cited a man who had kept his father's broken cameras hanging in the closet for years after his father had died. The writer called the man's grief unhealthy. But to me, keeping special belongings that characterize the person who has died is a way of taking that person into oneself. Traces of George are everywhere—his hairbrush in the bathroom, a jacket I particularly liked in the closet. I want to feel his presence and when I move on I want to take him with me.

Oh, no. Not now. The water pours into my bath. Bone-chilling cold. I know there is a way to restart the hot water heater but I have no idea what it is. It was always George who disappeared into the cellar, lantern in hand, to turn it back on. I call Lewis, who used to work for George. He directs me to a little button about two feet from the floor, just to the right of the furnace.

"You want me to come over?" he asks.

"No, no. I can find it," I reply, with more assurance than I feel.

The cellar is dark and damp, low-ceilinged, the old-fashioned kind that consists only of foundation and cracked concrete floor, the kind where unknown alien things lurk in shrouded corners, ready to attack when one's back is turned.

I descend slowly, closing the door behind me, grimacing as I push the cobwebs away from my face. Green weeds shoot out of the thin layer of soil that has seeped in to coat the sloping stone sills of the two small windows. I skulk toward the furnace, hunched over, to keep from cracking my head against the overhead beams and to avoid the endless cobwebs that, even so, brush against my hair. I look two feet from the floor, just to the right of the furnace. I hate it down here. Is that a button? I push. Nothing happens. I look again and see it—bright red, elongated, on top of a metal box. I press it and hear the ripple of flame coming alight in the furnace. Thank goodness.

I turn back toward the stairs, pleased to have mastered this small area of home maintenance. Somehow the cellar seems less alien now. I've penetrated its entire length and the water heats behind me.

Six columns support the overhead beams. I stare at them, one and then another. They are maroon, metal, with a threaded extension under a square plate at the top. Someone must have added them after the house was built. Was it because the beams weren't strong enough to support its weight? The chill encircles my throat and lifts the skin behind my ears. In that moment it occurs to me that the house may simply fall down.

"The house has been standing for eighty-eight years. It's not going to fall down now." Gail is a very good friend and I want to believe her, but she doesn't know any more about houses than I do. Still, I try to persuade myself that she is right.

Later in the day, Lewis comes by to see how I am getting along. He is retired now, but was so fond of George I think he feels he should watch out for me. A short, sturdy man with an eager smile, he is profoundly Christian. His impulses are always kind. But his faith is his own. He neither judges nor proselytizes.

I tell him I've almost finished unpacking fifty cartons of books.

"Fifty!" he exclaims. "Man, oh man." He puts his hands on his hips. "Fifty cartons of books. Man! You're adding a lot of weight to that house!" He chuckles.

Why does he say that?

"Too much?" I ask.

"Nah," he replies.

But I am unnerved again. Does he know something that I don't? Why is he grinning?

We leave the garage and stroll back toward the house. The wind ruffles the trees and he looks up, then says to me, "You'll need new gutters next year."

I look up at the gutters. They are the flat wooden kind that are really an extension of the roof. They seem no worse to me than the rest of the house.

"How can you tell?" I ask.

"Just look at your soffits," he replies.

I know no more than I did before, but if I won't need them until next year they can wait. I want desperately to ask him if he thinks the house might fall down, but I am embarrassed to put that question to a man.

"Do I need anything else?" I ask.

"Nah. You're fine otherwise."

"The house is sound?"

"Oh, yeah. The house is sound. The electric is good. You've got a new septic. You're in good shape."

I don't press the point, but cling to his assurance. At the same time I can't help but notice a whole class of what I know as adjectives being used as nouns. The other day the phone installer told me, "You've got a lot of poison back there." He meant poison ivy.

I never had nightmares before George died. Most of the one last night was unfocused, meandering, not particularly memorable. There was a lot of going back and forth between the entrance to our apartment building and the bistro on the opposite corner of Madison Avenue, but it is the intersection itself—the expanse of street, the lines of the curb—that lingers in my mind. I felt vaguely anxious, but didn't know why and didn't give it much thought. Finally, back in our apartment, I opened the door to a walk-in closet. The light was on. At my feet, dressed in a white shirt and navy trousers, George lay in a fetal position, palms pressed against his temples, jaw clenched, body shaking in an agony of pain. I woke up, sitting bolt upright in the bed, stifling a scream.

It is six months since George died and I am still reliving his death. We often went across the street for chicken salad or quiche, and as age made George less sure of foot, the street and the curb became real obstacles. On the morning of his heart attack he wore a white shirt and navy trousers to the hospital. He wasn't shaking with it but he was in terrible pain. The doctors gave him a shot of morphine and when it didn't help gave him another. It simply made him vomit. I can't get over how transparent the dream was. The horror of it has burrowed into me and in unguarded moments I feel the knife blade next to my heart.

Jesus! I used to enjoy thunderstorms but good Lord! The walls of the house are so thin. They sound brittle. With each crack of thunder I expect to hear them break. In the kitchen, water oozes through the Dutch door and around the glass in the windows. The sump pump clanks valiantly against the ever-rising tide of water in the cellar. Every few minutes I walk partway down the stairs with a flashlight to see how deep the water is. In New York we lived in fortresses but here I am naked. Mother Nature will do whatever she pleases with me. I wonder if I should have lightning rods. Is there such a thing as lightning rods anymore? I remind myself that the house has been here since 1900 and that lightning hasn't hit it yet. Maybe lightning doesn't hit houses anymore.

"Did you hear about Barney?" a customer in work clothes asks the proprietor of the newsstand. "His house got hit by lightning last night." Oh, no. I don't want to hear this. I plunk down my thirty cents for the paper, and after hearing enough to deduce that Barney's house didn't burn to the ground, bolt for the door.

George always used to say, "The worst never happens." My inevitable retort was "The worst does happen. It just doesn't happen to you."

He did seem to lead a life of narrow escapes. Heading back from Maine, in the summer of 1940, all went well until over Saddle River, New Jersey, he suddenly lost oil pressure in his Fairchild 24. The engine in the three-seater monoplane would seize up at any moment. He had to get the plane to the ground.

"Isn't that a nice farm down there," he remarked, not

wanting to frighten his son Dick, who was traveling with him and was ten years old at the time. "Why don't we go down and call on the owners."

After a perfect landing, he taxied to the end of the field, only to be met by the farmer, who was less than pleased at the damage that had been done to his corn crop. (He was even less pleased when a Stearman biplane, assuming that the field was a landing strip, made its own perfect landing a few moments later.) But his sense of injury was alleviated when George insisted on reimbursing him.

During his takeoff a week later, after the oil line had been repaired, George hit a rock, blowing his right tire. It was too late to abort the takeoff and he was soon high in the air with only one tire (the plane was a tail-dragger, but one touches down on the two forward wheels). Landing, for anyone, requires a certain skill, but for George, who had no depth perception, it could be difficult. He decided to land not at his home airport but at one with a longer runway nearby, and for insurance headed for the grass next to the runway rather than for the runway itself. He banked the plane to the left and, as gently as he could, set it down on its left wheel, then pulled back hard on the stick to slam down the tail. The plane righted itself, fell onto the other wheel, took one mighty spin, and, without turning over, settled to a stop. No harm done.

One hot summer day, when he was six or seven, George and the son of one of the men who worked in the stable reached an agreement over the single stick of gum they had between them. The boy folded it into his mouth and chewed it for a while, then gave it to George, who chewed it until long after the flavor was gone. That night the doctor was called to the boy's bedside. He had polio. George never got it.

I, on the other hand, have every confidence that the worst not only does, but probably will, happen. And hardly without reason. There is always some disease to think about, a plane crash. Unaware of a gas leak, a man on Long Island lights a cigarette and blows up his house.

Bad things did happen to George. His father was an alcoholic who, after a second marriage, disinherited him. Never a scholar, he flunked out of Princeton, thus coming up short in a family of scholars, and in a social world which he had been brought up to overvalue, which he was part of, but in which he would never be completely comfortable. Both parents, his mother if only by her superior native abilities, humiliated and demeaned him when he was young.

What is important is that he let nothing defeat him. Obstacles became a challenge, physical limitations inconveniences to be outwitted or ignored. The worst never happens if you don't let it be the worst.

George was a lucky man. But I wonder sometimes if we don't in many ways make our own luck. "The worst never happens." It worked for him. Maybe it will work for me.

The township Municipal Building is a modern, single-story, I-shaped building whose longitudinal axis runs parallel to the county road, and whose façade consists of sections of brick alternating with large double windows above white wooden panels. The top of the I is the head-quarters of the township police and the bottom a large meeting room in which this morning I can glimpse the last row of participants in the township exercise program. They step forward and back, forward and back, swinging their arms forward with each forward step, then back with each step back. After a short set they stop to rest. It seems to me a most unchallenging class, and one young woman, I would guess barely out of her teens, shoots me a look of embarrassed annoyance at being observed by an outsider.

I have been directed to an office just short of Police Headquarters where I will be able to register to vote, and I wait happily in the air-conditioned, blue-carpeted hallway. When her colleague leaves, the municipal clerk, a pleasant woman with short-cropped dark hair, motions me to a chair in her surprisingly spacious office. She takes my name and address, asks where I voted previously, and promises that my voting card will be in the mail in less than two weeks. That was easy. On the way out, I stop again at the information desk to ask about recycling and about the county well-testing program. They tell me that the recycling center is just beyond what I hear as Pickle Park, and I suppress an urge to come up with some remark about pickles. I step out into the sun with two fliers explaining the recycling program and a plastic tote bag containing a copy of "The Clean Water Book," two pages of information on the Watershed Association Well Test Program, a sheet of instructions on how to take a water sample, and a plastic-wrapped, clear plastic sample cup, with lid. Samples are to be delivered to the Municipal Building on August 23rd.

Already I feel more a part of this place, this life. Later, as I stand in the kitchen, washing dishes, looking out through the open Dutch door, I realize that a house is home in a way an apartment never can be and I relish the sense of belonging that I feel in this house of my own.

Clearly, I don't see my house as others see it. Art Hart is here to show me how to repack the pumps on my Stanley Steamer. After a quick sandwich in the house at lunchtime, we step out of the dining room onto the side section of porch and his mouth curves in a trace of a smile.

"This house is in pretty tough shape," he says. He wraps his hand around one of the porch posts.

The alarm goes off in my head again, as I respect Art's engineering ability above anyone's. He works for Bell Labs and has an impeccable Stanley of his own.

"It'd cost a fortune to fix this porch. All the paint would have to be scraped. I'm not even sure you'd find somebody willing to do it."

Needless to say, it is not peeling paint that worries me, but whether he thinks the house will fall down. Again I am embarrassed to ask.

"You know what Bud said," he adds with a grin.

Bud is a mutual friend, a building contractor, who did some work in the house for George before we moved in.

"Promise you won't tell him I told you. He said, 'Why doesn't George just tear down that damned house and start over?' " He laughs.

I can't help but recall that when Bud was thumping and chipping around a doorframe an avalanche of plaster fell on his head. Surely that had some bearing on his assessment of the house. On the other hand, the plaster did fall on his head, which suggests a certain lack of soundness.

"Do you think I'm foolish to try to stay here?" This is the closest I can come to asking if he thinks the house will fall down.

"Do you like the layout?" he asks dubiously.

I am a little hurt. It is the inside of the house that pleases me.

"The layout is fine. Especially for only one person." Perhaps the fact that we use the side and not the front door as a main entrance makes the layout seem less classic than it is.

"Then I'd stick it out. The lot's on a corner. Someday

this area will be zoned commercial and the place will be worth a lot of money."

"Would anyone want to buy the house?"

"They'd buy it for the land and pull the house down, put up a 7-Eleven or something."

"I'll put up my own 7-Eleven," I declare, refusing to acknowledge my clearly unenviable position.

"There you go," he replies.

If he thinks I can wait until I'm allowed to put up a 7-Eleven, he doesn't think the house will fall down just yet. After he leaves, I sit in an overstuffed chair in the living room—with its hunting prints, the old books in the bookcase, the Chippendale-style sofa—and I wonder a bit wistfully why my house seems to have positive attributes only for me.

When George died people assumed that I had expected it. Some even said, though not to me, "Oh, well, she must have known it was coming." As though knowing it was coming meant that I would feel no pain. Others said, "He hadn't been very well," in a tone that suggested there was some justice in his death.

The fact is that, subconsciously, I thought George would never die. I had grown accustomed to his rallying. During a nearly fatal bout with septicemia in the seventies, he lost his equilibrium, and when he was finally well enough to go out, we would walk side by side along busy New York streets. I would be saying something to him and suddenly he would be gone, careering behind me in a dizzying swath that would lead to a lamppost or a mailbox, where he would catch himself to keep from falling. But he kept at it until he was well.

In Paris, a couple of months before he died, he woke at 3:00 A.M. in our little Left Bank hotel, vomiting blood from what proved to be a bleeding ulcer. The Paris ambulance drivers carried him delirious down four narrow flights of stairs and in their shining Citroën ambulance took him to Cochin Hospital, where, after several nearly successful attempts to scale the rails of the bed, he lay agitated and disoriented, then sank into a weakness so profound I thought he might be slipping away. On the fifth day, I approached his room, dreading what I would find, only to see him out of bed, sitting at a table, wolfing down steak and *pommes frites,* joking with the nurses. They understood none of his English but smiled happily at his good cheer. He was known throughout the hospital as *"celui qui parle anglais"*—the one who speaks English.

This last time, in the emergency room, after the cardiologist explained the results of his tests, I said, "What you are telling me is that he might die." I choked on the words. But I knew that she didn't know what I knew—that George always came back.

A young friend once asked, "Tell me the truth. Don't

you ever wish that some night he would just go peacefully to sleep and never wake up?" By that time he was having equilibrium problems again. His eyesight was bad. He had gotten older. But I never wished that. Regardless of his health he was the center of my life. I loved him, depended on him, and I wanted him with me forever.

I can't believe it. I just can't believe it.

It is after midnight. Rain thrashes the brittle walls of my house. Thunder roars in the darkness. It is late for me. I stand by the doorway between the dining room and the kitchen, transfixed as bulbous globs of rainwater ooze out of a crack above my head and then, too heavy, break loose and plummet into a pool slowly spreading across the floor. How can this be? What am I doing here? The house is nothing but a sieve.

I go to the laundry room for a bucket and rags. I have to do something, call someone. But who? What? I place the bucket under the worst of the falling water and watch as the clump of rags absorbs the puddle on the floor. Bud will never come to help me. He hates this house. But I can't just pretend this never happened. Who knows how much of the house has rotted already?

The water oozes overhead. I have never felt so exposed, or so alone.

All right. So Bud won't come to my house. He must know someone who would. The following evening I dial his number. I could be wrong. Maybe he will come. His wife Carol answers the phone. I tell her I need someone to fix my leak, but, equally important, someone to look over the entire house and tell me if it is sound. I don't want to put them in an awkward position so I ask if Bud might recommend someone.

"Bud would do it himself," she replies too hastily, "but he's so busy."

So I was right the first time. He won't come. Carol doesn't even call him to the phone. But she is friendly. She tells me they'll try to think of someone and call me back. I've done all I can do for the moment. Now I'll just have to wait.

George and I met at dinner. I had just come to New York from Wyoming, where we had moved when I was seventeen, to find a job in publishing, and a friend of mine had telephoned a cousin, who worked in publishing, for advice.

"Come tomorrow night for dinner," she told him.

"George Schieffelin will be there. He's Executive Vice President of Scribners."

Ever naïve, I felt uncomfortable with what I regarded as pulling strings. I wanted to get a job in the personnel office, not at the dinner table. But I agreed to go.

We rode up in the elevator with a convivial group who, it was soon apparent, were guests at the same dinner. Among them was a man in a navy topcoat, with thick, formerly black, now almost completely white hair, combed back on a diagonal from his finely sculpted, yet slightly rugged, face. He looked steadily at me, with interest, but without a word, as the others chatted. I looked back, holding his gaze. In that look, each of us said to the other—I know who you are, you know who I am, and the others, caught up in their talk, know nothing.

I was seated at his left at dinner. The deep mahogany of the table shone beneath white lace place mats and Sèvres service plates. He leaned back in his chair, blue-sleeved forearms extended forward on the table, the cuffs of his blue-striped shirt crisp at his wrists beyond his coatsleeves. The strong, slender fingers of his right hand toyed lightly with the stem of his water glass. After a few words with our hostess he turned to me.

"I hear you're looking for a job," he said.

"That's right," I replied. My hands were in my lap.

"What do you want to do?" he asked.

He had given me my cue. Now I was to talk about my

love of ideas, my passion for books, my dream of living in New York, where books and ideas thrived. I was certainly not supposed to state directly what we all already knew—that I wanted him to give me a job.

"Work for a publisher," I replied. I didn't like this game. And I had taken his measure. I knew I could "cut the nonsense" (as he would have said) and get away with it. He would think it was funny.

The table froze. No one spoke. No one moved. The air bristled with my impropriety. It was for him to offer, not for me to demand. What would he do?

He gave me a quizzical look. Then he burst out laughing. Everyone at the table relaxed, and laughed. The danger had passed.

E ver naïve, I thought I had the job.

"Are you interested in ideas?" he had asked.

"Yes."

"Can you type?"

"Yes." This was a slight enhancement of my abilities, as I had only just finished a course in typing at the Northern Wyoming Community College.

He told me they needed an assistant to the Managing Editor of a reference project called the *Dictionary of the History of Ideas.*

I telephoned at ten the next morning, as he had suggested.

"Oh, yes," he said, after I identified myself. "I've told
Miss Adair about you. Just a moment while I transfer you."

Apparently, I didn't have the job after all. Mr. Schieffelin was one of the owners. Miss Adair, the personnel director,
would see me in two days.

Miss Adair was quite young, and not friendly. She took every
opportunity to challenge my qualifications. I, confident that
I could do anything I put my mind to, was too ignorant of
the business world to be intimidated. She asked about my
office experience. I told her I had been director of the Sheri-
dan County Republican Headquarters during the presiden-
tial campaign the previous fall.

"So you've never worked in an office," she said.

"I *ran* one," I countered.

"Can you type?"

"Yes." She never gave me a typing test.

Toward the end of the interview she asked, "Where did
you meet Mr. Schieffelin?"

"At dinner," I replied.

She waited expectantly for the rest of the story. I figured
I'd already told her more than she needed to know and said
nothing.

Years later, George told me he'd eavesdropped on the
entire interview, and I delighted in the image of him snoop-

ing on the other side of the partition and in the pleasure I knew he would have felt at my standing my ground.

Two days and still no word from Bud. Or Carol. Can it be so difficult to find someone willing *just to look* at my house? I tell myself that the house is probably in better condition than I think. But what if it isn't?

This morning I take my first trip to the recycling center, driving past what turns out to be Pickel Park (for Baltus Pickel, a local eighteenth-century landowner), then up a steep slope to the left, and through the open gates of a tall, chain link fence. Facing me is a huge metal shed that resembles an airplane hangar, and directly to its right the open end of a semitrailer whose interior is piled high with newspapers. I have tied my newspapers and magazines in separate bundles, with a knot that I hope the authorities will find satisfactory. (The fliers specify a cake-box tie or a package knot, but I'm not sure what those are.) After climbing the shallow wooden steps to the back of the trailer and depositing both bundles, I return to my car and survey the series of wooden sections that parallel the side of the shed. Each is approximately twenty feet wide by forty feet deep. The ones for glass are labeled: BROWN-GLASS, GREEN-GLASS, CLEAR-GLASS. The brown section glistens with empty beer bottles, the green with mineral water and wine, the clear with whiskey bottles and mayonnaise jars. The section for aluminum cans is brash with the red of Classic Coke, the green of Sprite, the silver of Bud and Coors Light.

The appliances have long since overflowed their compartment. Much-used stoves, dishwashers, washing machines, the doorless hulks of old refrigerators tilt hectically, higher and higher. There is something otherworldly about the hot water heater that virtually alone stands upright, like a quiet sentinel. On the ground nearby is a large, black bowling ball. Such a cliché, this, the detritus of modern industrial life. I am told that however worthy the idea, there is little market for recycled materials. These endlessly growing mountains of cans and bottles, refrigerators and stoves. How they diminish us.

One of the reasons that George and I were drawn to one another is that, as I phrased it to myself at the time, we had the same sense of style. We took pleasure in things left unsaid. On the most obvious level, I think of his taking me into the editorial floor library after I had been hired. He flung one leg over the arm of his chair, twirling his glasses by an earpiece as he explained my role in keeping the *Dictionary of the History of Ideas* on track. He was in midsentence when his glasses shot out of his hand, flew across the book-lined room, banged into a shelf of books, and crashed to the carpeted floor. He looked over his shoulder, appraised the situation, and with no change of expression turned back and went on talking.

It was so often like that. We were the detached observers. No human foible, no transgression, surprised us. We saw the same things, had the same response, bubbled with the same internal laughter, and without saying a word knew we were thinking the same thing and reveled in our shared unspoken secret.

On a deeper level, we simply didn't labor things. We read each other and accommodated. I think we both sensed that if a relationship had to be worked at, there was something unworkable about it. I can't say that this lasted forever, or that accommodation was always so simple. But it was during only one period that those unspoken leaps of understanding became impossible. Early on, George said to me, "I feel as though we've known each other for three hundred years. Being with you is like coming home." I felt the same way.

Four days. Still no word from Bud or Carol. Have they forgotten? Should I call again? I couldn't have missed them. When I go out, even if it's just to dump the garbage, I turn on the answering machine. Maybe there's something wrong with my machine. I drive to the A & P and call myself from the pay phone to test it. It seems to work. Maybe they just refuse to talk to machines. This morning a friend of George's, who used to be the mayor, told me cheerfully that I'd never find anyone. They're all too busy. At least I've gotten one thing done. Lewis has found me someone to cut the shrubbery. But what am I supposed to do about the house? Sit here while it crumbles around my ears?

These nightmares! Giant tropical plants with fronds like elephant ears laced through the rats' nest of planks that blocked my path. I had waited too long. The sky was darkening. In a moment night would fall and I would be lost. I gathered my belongings and pressed forward, pushing desperately at a plank that refused to budge. I awakened with books, papers, the telephone cradled in my arms, feeling my way around the foot of my heavy Victorian bed. I didn't know where I was.

When I tell people about this dream I laugh, as if to suggest that it was funny. But it wasn't funny. I lay back on the bed in the black heat of the summer night and waited for my heart to burst, as it pounded, with terrifying force but no weight, a toy hammer, against my chest. The electric fan whirred in the darkness. The trucks roared by, oblivious.

Finally, a name. Carol has called and suggested Pete Malone, who is restoring a house down the road. "You know, the white one with all the cornice brackets," she says. I don't know, but at this point I'll talk to anyone. When I call he says he will come tomorrow. I can scarcely contain my gratitude. Not only is he willing to come, but he has offered to come right away. I wonder if he has understood that I am afraid.

Pete Malone is a big man, tall, an outsize Robert Benchley, in madras shorts and street shoes. He arrives at 11:00 A.M. and when I greet him by his surname he interrupts robustly, "Pete." After the formality of New York, I am uneasy with this immediate familiarity, but that is the way here. I tell him again what has alarmed me about the house and am finally able to admit, albeit jokingly, as though I really know there is no chance of it, that I am afraid it might fall down.

He steps back off the porch and surveys the house from between two ragged sections of boxwood. I watch his eyes travel over the thick, gray-tinged, peeling paint of the porch, the screen doors gaping from their hinges. I begin to see the house as he must see it. His eyes stop briefly at the baked-out porch roof, once rectangular shingles now crumbling encrustations atop another layer crumbling in its turn. Back on the porch, he pulls himself up onto the railing and taps his knuckle along the underside of the roof, indicating which boards are rotten, then steps down and follows the porch around to the front of the house. He points out that as there are already two layers of shingles, it would be against the building code to add another.

"You might get away with adding a third," he says. "You wouldn't really have to apply for a permit."

He gazes at another rotten plank.

"Whether the porch would fall down, I don't know."

I grin at his joke.

After a quick tour of the inside of the house, he suggests I get in touch with Bob Beck, a general contractor who will be able to tell me, board by board, what is sound and what isn't.

As he pulls out of the driveway, I think again of his remark about the porch falling down. It *was* a joke, wasn't it? I try to recapture the moment in which he made it. But there is no answer there.

Bob Beck can't come until Monday! It's only Wednesday now. In my mind's eye, I see the porch breaking loose from the house and, all rotting planks and posts and splinters, collapsing to the ground. I tell myself not to worry so much. It may not fall down for a month or two. And even if it does, chances are it won't fall *on* anyone. But what if it does? What if it falls on the UPS man, for example? Not only will I be responsible for his death, but his widow will sue me for forty million dollars and I'll spend the rest of my working life trying to earn enough money to pay her off. Five days until Monday. I can scarcely bring myself to leave the premises, for fear that if I do, the porch will cave in on the first delivery man to come to the door. Five days! How am I going to get through five days?

Once George's funeral was over and the family had dispersed, I was alone. It was a relief to have them gone. I could give up the ordeal of maintaining a civil exterior, of forcing back the pain in my heart. While they had been with me, I had had, again and again, to disappear when I could no longer hold back the tears, to sob silently in some other room. We ate in restaurants, and inevitably during the meal, the pressure would build up inside of me until I was nauseated, claustrophobic, my nerves like sounding cello strings. I had to force myself to smile across the gulf that separated them from me.

Occasionally, even when they were still there, the tension dissipated. Murray distinguished himself by escaping out the back door of our apartment and, in the fewer than ten seconds it took for me to grab him, began to pee beside the neighbors' doormat. I ran for paper towels and Fantastik, wiped up the mess, and, on my hands and knees, breathed hugely to see if I had gotten all the smell. Then I saw the considerably larger pool that was poised to flow under their door. Frantic, I wiped and scrubbed, sniffed, nose to the floor, hoping that none of it had trickled inside (these neighbors would not be amused), hoping they wouldn't catch me on my knees, sniffing at their door. He had been out for less than ten seconds! He had never been out before. How had he developed such singleness of purpose so quickly? My account of this near calamity reduced us all to helpless, giddy laughter. For days afterward, I would tiptoe to the neighbors' door, leaning down, sniffing, to see if there was any lingering evidence of Murray's territoriality.

Alone, I sank into an exhaustion that lasted for weeks. I could do one chore per day. Pay a bill. Write a note. Usually right after breakfast. Then I would be so tired that I could do nothing but sit, or putter aimlessly, for the rest of the morning. Curled under a quilt, I would sleep all afternoon.

I gathered my circumscribed world around me like a cocoon. Wanting to be alone to be with George, I saw virtually no one. With those I did see, I talked endlessly of him. I read English mysteries. I felt safe in a structured universe in which there were rules. It was fortunate that I had quit my job the previous spring. I would have been incapable of going to work.

The biggest intrusion was the fundraisers, the worst, the gun people, the Citizens' Committee for the Right to Keep and Bear Arms, the Second Amendment Foundation. The caller would ask to speak to George and I would be unable to bring myself to reveal to someone who, for me, was simply some young gunslinger the agonizing, private fact of his death. I asked one woman simply to drop him from their mailing list.

"I'd like to talk to Mr. Schieffelin personally," she insisted.

"I'm afraid that won't be possible."

"I can't do anything without Mr. Schieffelin's okay. When is the best time to reach him?"

"There is no best time."

"Why not?"

"Because he's dead."

"Oh well," she says, "that's different. Why didn't you say so?" Now she is satisfied.

"I go out for the day, and by the time I get back the wisteria has grown over the door. I have to tear it loose to get inside. What's worse, it's full of big black ants that bite."

Ed Lanza laughs. He and his men have arrived with a one-ton Ford dump truck, a three-quarter-ton heavy-duty pickup, a John Deere tractor, with Brush Hog, on a flatbed trailer, and an assortment of hand mowers, clippers, sprayers, hedge trimmers, chain saws, a pole trimmer, and chains. All this to contain my shrubbery.

Ed is a large teddy bear of a man, with patches of gray in his close-cropped dark beard and flecks of gray in his hair. He has a warm, sweet smile and an unassuming gallantry that I find charming.

He repeats his tour of a few days before, when he came to give me an estimate, and explains what he intends to do. I follow him to the back of the house, where a cracked concrete walk disappears at the merge point of a towering mass of forsythia and the holly tree. He pushes his way through, and holds back a holly branch for me to pass. We are surrounded now, holly and forsythia behind, and ahead, a semicircle of tall, full pines, whose lower limbs reach outward eight to ten feet, even at the level of our knees. A privet hedge arching high in the background closes us into a humid, almost Stygian gloom.

By the holly tree, a birdbath, once part of a fountain, rises out of a concrete basin embedded in the ground. Where birds once splashed, there is only a narrow steel pipe, extending upward without purpose. Ed warns me not to step into the groundhog hole that lurks, a foot in diameter, just under the forsythia. This is apparently the groundhog's main entrance, as we discover other smaller holes nearby.

I warn Ed, in turn, not to drive his tractor into the ditch that Lewis tells me runs from the far side of the house toward the garage. As it is hidden by thick, tall grass, and I seldom venture on that side of the house in any event, I have not seen it in its entirety, but I show him the end closest to the garage. It is about a foot deep.

"That's no problem," he says.

It is late in the landscaping season and we agree that he will simply cut back this year. Next year we'll worry about aesthetics. Somehow Ed's presence makes it easier to wait for Bob Beck. He sets to work and I leave for New York to go to the dentist.

I was lucky in one way when George died. From the beginning I could cry. Lynn Caine told in *Widow* of not having been able to cry after her husband's death. Even well into the writing of her book, she hadn't cried for him. After a heart-wrenching account of the death of her husband Moss Hart, Kitty Carlisle says in *Kitty,* "I didn't cry. Tears were for pinpricks, not for tragedy. I was dry-eyed and empty." Others have spoken of the numbness that helps one get through the days immediately following a death.

I never felt numb. And looking back, I am grateful to have experienced the pain right away, to have had the outlet of tears, to have experienced George's dying to the fullest. My problem was to keep from crying. The Saturday after the funeral, I sobbed through the entire Metropolitan Opera broadcast of *Pelléas*. (Many would argue that some form of desperation is an entirely normal human response to *Pelléas*, regardless of the circumstances.) I had to give up calling people to let them know that George had died. I would tell them the news and hear the sharp intake of breath and the silence, while they collected themselves, tried to think of something to say. It finally became too much for me. That gasp. That pause. Their concern for me.

I put on mascara for the funeral. I told myself it would help me not to cry. I didn't want rivulets of black trailing down my face. While I was waiting in an aisle behind the altar before the service, someone handed me a copy of the program the church had prepared. I looked down and saw the headline: "Service of Thanksgiving for the Life of George McKay Schieffelin." Thanksgiving. A giving of thanks for the joy of sharing his life. Seldom has the language of the church seemed so apt to me. It made his life an entity, a part of the universe, a part of time. A blessing. I had lost him. And in the pain, I had not thought to be grateful for his life. We were all here together to give thanks. Reminding myself of the mascara, I beat back the tears.

Ed is just pulling out of the driveway when I return, his truck piled high with forsythia, grass cuttings, the top six feet of a maple tree. He lets me pass, then backs his truck, cuts the motor, and jumps down out of the cab. He seems eager to tell me something.

"I think I know why your cellar leaks," he says.

He leads me along the far side of the house, eyes on the foundation, then lowers himself onto one knee. The grass has been cut and I can see why he has stopped. The kitchen and the laundry room are a single-story box tacked onto the back of the house. By the crawl space under the laundry room I see the near edge of a cavernous hole.

"It's an old cistern," he says.

I peer inside and see the sloping brick lining, much of it still intact.

"I bet this is where the rain gets in. If we close it off and build up the soil along the foundation, I think your cellar will stay dry."

He shifts himself a few feet to the right where the soil has eroded to reveal a section of pipe.

"I found something else too. This here's a septic drain. It must have frozen last winter." He shows me the break in its underside. "You'll have to get a plumber to put in a new one."

I hardly dare think what may have spilled out of that pipe.

"Will it just freeze again?"

"Maybe. But when we build up the soil, it will be better protected."

He stands and turns to the newly cut grass. For the first time I notice the wide seam of fill dirt that reaches outward toward the garage.

"You know that ditch?" he says.

"Yes."

"You know how deep it was?"

"How deep?"

"Four feet! It's a good thing I was driving forward, not back. I would have gone right into it." He grins. He seems to regard hidden four-foot-deep ditches as one of the inevitable hazards of life, but I am dizzy with the idea of him tipping over on 4,000 pounds of tractor.

"I got three loads of dirt and filled it right in."

I can't take my eyes off the arc of New Jersey red shale.

"Well, I'd better be going," he says. He starts toward his truck. "What do you have in the garage?"

"My husband was an antique-car collector. I still have three of his cars. Well, the Stanley Steamer was mine."

"You have a Stanley Steamer!?"

"Mmm. Maybe you'd like to see it sometime."

"I sure would."

"We'll do it tomorrow."

He waves goodbye. I wave back, my mind tossing with images of the ditch, the cistern, the break in the septic drain. I feel leaden under the weight of these things I know nothing about.

I must see if there are any more holes. Before someone tips over a tractor. Or simply falls. I reconnoitre the lot in parallel rows and scribble the location of each hole I find on the back of an envelope: "Across driveway, opposite middle porch post; opposite second telephone pole from the county road; under second wisteria bush from corner; under spruce tree, twenty feet from sump drain." In one particularly lumpy area, I discover a section of electric wiring, emerging from then burrowing back under the ground. The tractor has probably run over it, as the glint of copper wire alternates on the same plane with the black of crushed insulation. Is there no end to this? What if some child chases his ball onto my lawn? I cover the wire with a large, flat rock. The house is out of control. And I begin to think it has the power to destroy.

When I first see Ed the next morning, he is tearing honeysuckle off of the boxwood. He reaches over the boxwood at chest level and grabs hold with canvas-gloved hands, then braces himself and hauls in the tenacious, sinuous vines. He laughs when I tell him I have catalogued all the holes and promises to bring more dirt to fill them in. I warn him about the wire.

One of Ed's men wraps a chain around the base of the honeysuckle bush and fastens it to the drawbar of the tractor. Looking over his shoulder, he inches the tractor forward. I wince inwardly at the popping, cracking, of roots being torn asunder, the sound like muted artillery fire. When he finishes, there is a gaping, root-lined cavity in the dusty soil, and I feel a sense of loss in spite of the fact that the honeysuckle was overrunning and strangling other shrubs and trees.

Late in the day, when the others have left, I suggest to Ed that we have a look at the cars.

"A Stanley Steamer!" he exclaims, his face alight at the sight of the Stanley. "I've heard the name, but I never really knew they existed. I sure never dreamed I'd ever see one!"

The Stanley is red, with yellow axles and yellow wheels, its fenders and the molding on its wooden carriage body black, accented with yellow striping. The lamps—head, side, and rear—are made of brass.

"What year is it?"

"Nineteen-oh-nine."

He rounds the car and his eyes fix on the word "Stanley," rising on a diagonal, in two-and-a-half-inch brass script, on the front of the "coffin-nose" hood.

"And it runs on steam," he marvels.

"It's sort of like a gas stove," I tell him. "There's a pilot light, and a main burner. The main burner heats the water to make steam and the steam powers the engine." I show him the boiler under the hood, the burner pan under the boiler, the fuel tanks—for the pilot on the running board, for the main burner under the rumble seat, the water tank under the divided front seat.

"How do you light the pilot?"

"Propane torch."

He gives me a look of surprised respect.

"And the engine?"

"Right here in front of the rear axle."

He peers under the car.

"How far can you go before you run out of water?"

"It depends on the terrain and how fast you're going. Twenty or thirty miles."

"Then what do you do when you run out?"

"Pull up to someone's house and ask to use the garden hose. Or if you come to a stream or pond, you can use the siphon hose." I unfasten the leather apron above the running board to show him the rose-colored, twenty-five-foot siphon hose.

"How fast can it go?"

"Oh, sixty easily."

"Sixty!"

"It can go faster, but without a windshield or roof, sixty seems fast enough."

"Does it have gears?"

"No, you just open the throttle. The wider you open it the faster you go. It's like a steam locomotive. The steam from the exhaust goes chumf-a-chumf-a-chuff-a-chuff-a-chuff-a-chuff-a. What's interesting is that a steam locomotive runs on about two hundred pounds of steam pressure. The Stanley runs on six hundred."

"And you drive it yourself?"

"Mmm."

I tell him briefly about the other cars, but it is the Stanley that captivates him, as it does me.

"A Stanley Steamer!" He runs one hand along the curve of a fender. "Beautiful." He pronounces it byoo-dee-ful.

I am delighted with his response. The car is one of George's greatest gifts to me and I relate to it almost as if it were alive.

Mariah eats cobwebs. I heard her first, the snapping of her jaws, the moist, rapid-fire click of tongue against palate. She emerged from behind a curtain licking her chops, cobwebs clinging to her whiskers, smeared across her face. I wondered why she wasn't losing any weight. I've had her on a diet. Granted, she hardly moves in this heat. But cobwebs are protein, aren't they?

Thursday evening. Three days until Bob Beck comes. I have called the plumber about the septic drain. Lewis knows an electrician who has done some work on the house. He will ask him to check the wire. I sit on the porch steps at the side of the house, arms around my knees, in the still air of the summer evening. A hot-air balloon, in a jacquard pattern of fuchsia, soft green, blue, passes overhead. Three more days.

It was George who was the heart of Scribners when I arrived. He would make his rounds, from desk to desk, office to office, stopping to chat, in no hurry, the bright white of his hair set off against the gray or blue of his English-tailored suit, the straight cut of his shoulders suggesting he was someone to rely on. Though on the short side, he was larger than life, as I saw him, against the background of tall oak paneling that formed the offices on the editorial floor. He had the ease of a man who was where he knew he belonged. As a child, he had accompanied his uncle, the architect Ernest Flagg, to the building site at 48th Street and Fifth Avenue, as construction began on the exquisite Beaux-Arts building that Flagg had designed to house the Scribner bookstore and publishing firm. Now, George was larger than life, but approachable, hands clasped behind his back as he strolled around the floor, expectant, a light in his hazel eyes. He was interested in everyone.

He was not all talk. He would stand sometimes for minutes, saying nothing, thinking—the kind of comfortable silences you knew you didn't have to fill. He came by them naturally. Meetings between Max Perkins and his Uncle Charlie Scribner were often silent.

"Max would walk into Charlie's office," George often recalled. "They'd nod at each other, then stand by the window, or face one another across the desk. Five minutes would go by and neither of them would say a word. Then Max would nod in agreement and go back to his office." George would grin with delight here. "They'd made their decision."

An exaggeration, perhaps, but essentially true.

Fran Reilly was a secretary, in her fifties, whose desk was near mine.

"He's such a cute man," she once said to me after George had stopped by. "For a woman my age, that is," she felt it necessary to explain.

George was not a linear thinker. And he often spoke in metaphors. So to say that we shared unspoken secrets is not to say that I always understood what he said. At least not at the beginning. No one did.

After dinner on the night that we met, he spoke to me at length, in his slightly hoarse voice, of fox hunting, his antique cars, publishing. His voice did not carry well, and it was difficult even to hear his occasional, what seemed to me somewhat cryptic, remarks. I simply reacted, I hoped appropriately, and stored the remark in the back of my mind to decipher later. Russell Duncan, his lawyer, tells laughingly of the first years in which he did work for George. He, too, puzzled over the cryptic remarks, fearing that George must think him an imbecile. Until George asked him to join the Scribner board.

The fact is that George made leaps one had to learn to fill in. If only I could think of an example. Though even if I could, it would be a little like the remark, thought so amusing at a party the night before, that falls flat in the cold light of morning. Oh well, here's an easy one. The connection was not always so clear as it is here, but it shows how the process worked.

George and I were watching the model Lauren Hutton in some grade B television thriller. I grew more and more dissatisfied, until finally I burst out: "Lauren Hutton is all wrong for this. She just isn't convincing. She's too thin." Without missing a beat, George said to me, "Go get some dessert." I'm probably even thinner than Lauren Hutton.

Sometimes, one tangential fact would send him off on a flight of imagination that would bring him back to the subject from an entirely different and entirely unexpected direction. When his sally landed on target, it came as a characteristic flash of insight, or wit. When it didn't, when the tangential fact was an insufficient basis for the assumptions of his imaginings, it tended to add to his mystique. The listener assumed it was he who was lacking. In either case, George kept everyone alert.

Friday night and I have no car. The Suburban is in the shop. Its computer is telling the fuel pump not to pump. The Rabbit won't shift into first gear, and the Volkswagen people tell me I'll ruin it if I start off in second. It's going to be a long weekend.

Saturday morning. Hot. I put on an old white T-shirt and a pair of khaki shorts, my Top-Siders. An entire weekend in this relentless heat. I feel a wave of self-pity. My two-and-a-half-acre plot of ground suddenly resembles a prison farm. And heat or no heat, away from the city, I am a true American—claustrophobic without a car. I look out the bedroom window at the sun beating down on the porch roof. There is only one answer—fire up the Stanley.

An inner voice reminds me that Lewis is at a motor home exhibit in the Poconos; Art is in Maine. I have never taken the Stanley out entirely alone. If I get into trouble, there is no one here to help.

"What's the worst thing that can happen?" I ask my inner voice.

"The vaporizer could fill up with carbon. The pumps might not function properly."

"I know what to do about that now."

"You could get a flat tire."

"So I'll pull off the road."

"And just leave the car?"

"I'll figure that out when it happens."

I open the garage door and the Stanley faces me, the sun just touching the brass script on its red metal hood. I slip my driver's license, the registration, and the insurance card under the black leather cushion of the driver's seat, then check the water gauge on the dash to be sure there is water in the boiler. With a wooden stick, I check the fuel levels, Coleman lantern fuel in the pilot tank, a mixture of diesel fuel and unleaded gas for the main burner. I stick my index finger into the tank under the floor of the front seat, bringing up the requisite inch and a half of thick, brown steam cylinder oil. I cringe a little as I grab for a paper towel to wipe it off.

Art has made me a #60 drill to clean the nozzle holes and a $1/8$-inch drill to clean the back of the fuel jets. I kneel down in front of the burner pan and with a $3/8$-inch wrench remove the jets and gently rotate the drills, then blow through the jets and hold them up to the light, before replacing them, to be sure they are free of carbon. With a screwdriver I remove the pilot needle and pull it through a fold of #600 sandpaper until the flat part of the needle is shiny.

Standing by the car on the driver's side, I release the emergency brake and push the car forward, catching it again with the brake before it bounds too far out of the garage. I light my propane torch and kneel in front of the car again to heat the pilot nozzle, the copper fuel line, and through the peek hole in the burner pan, the pilot burner itself. After two or three minutes, with the flame from the torch over the pilot, I open the pilot fuel valve. The pilot lights and I move the torch back to the nozzle area and the fuel line, which have been cooled by the sudden flow of raw fuel. The pilot flame seems to be lifting from the burner and I reduce the pressure in the fuel tank.

I relight the torch and heat the area around the main burner nozzles, then, at short intervals, crack the firing-up valve on the dash, before leaving it open to allow the more volatile pilot fuel to flow steadily through the main burner jets to the main burner. With the main burner preheated, I close the firing-up valve and, this time, crack the main burner valve several times, gently introducing the main fuel to the vaporizer, then leave it open. The fuel flows evenly and I climb into the passenger seat to pump up the fuel pressure and to watch the steam-pressure gauge for the first sign of steam. The needle moves at last, almost imperceptibly, off of "0," then slowly, 10, 20, 30, 40.

With steam pressure at 200 psi, I move the car slowly, forward and back, to clear water from the cylinders. With steam pressure at 400, I am ready to go.

The combination of sunscreen and perspiration drips down my face as I check the pilot once again. It is still lifting off the burner, but the pressure in the tank is low enough. I tell my inner voice that the worst it can do is to go out. Which creates a few puffs of acrid black smoke, but is not a crisis. I open the throttle on the steering column, chumf-a-chumf-a-chuff-a-chuff-a, and pull onto the county road.

The wind whips my hair. I open the throttle further and feel the gentle pressure of the seat on my back as I am propelled effortlessly faster. From the exhaust, a trail of steam pulses behind me. The speed limit is 50 mph and I keep up easily with the traffic, my eyes turning at frequent intervals to oil and water gauges, as I travel through a section of modern ranch-style houses, an area of woodland, more houses, then a large farm—tall, metal-domed silos beside a cluster of farm buildings, cattle grazing in a field. There is something cheerful, eager to please, in the bark of the exhaust as I open the throttle wider at the crest of a hill. At a crossroad I see what appears to be an old mill nestled against a stream bank. I turn off, past a general store, one side of the road dotted with white colonial farmhouses, on the other an expanse of pasture, descending into a valley, framed in the distance by soft green hills. The car is steaming well and I feel almost giddy, my body open to the wind, the sense that with one small leap I could fly. I close the throttle partway and chuff peaceably for a while, a farmer's wife in 1909. As I approach, I feel tempted to drive up the driveway to our former house, but continue on, back to the county road, the circle completed.

Back home, I refill the water tank and clean the fuel jets. This time they are hot and I can hold them only briefly, even with canvas gloves.

Septic drain, ditch, exposed electric wires loom less large now as I pull out of the driveway toward town. This is one of the reasons I am here—the beauty and power of this shining red machine, the sound of steam that somehow touches something in my soul.

Past the post office, the drugstore, Union Hotel, people wave from the sidewalk, toot their car horns in approval, at the sight of me. I pass the A & P and its mall, and turn briefly left, then right at the Exxon station, and several miles to another town, this one half a mile of Victorian houses, each different, each exuberant in design, a palette of colors: cream with Wedgwood blue shutters; yellow with forest green shutters, white trim; tan with dusty dark blue; salmon with white; medium brown with green; white. A riot of turrets, gables, fretwork, pointed Gothic windows.

At the far edge of town, the vista opens into a tree-rimmed valley, sectioned by cumulous hedgerows of wild roses. Coming toward me in an open Jeep is a young, stocky, bearded man—an outdoorsman, who, I decide by the look of him, reads Peter Matthiessen, Borges. He is ebullient at the sight of a lone woman in her Stanley Steamer and he gives me a thumbs-up sign and a broad grin. I pull the cord that runs along the steering column and my steam whistle sounds in the bright summer air. It all but lifts him out of his seat and he cries out with delight, "Bravo!"

I turn onto the narrow country road that George and I so often traveled in a modern car. The road dips in a curve to the left. The trees fall away to reveal another stream, a pasture beyond, and in the distance a large white colonial house. I feel George over my shoulder, hands in his pockets, happy, proud, watching me. I see myself as he must see me, from behind, wind whipping my hair, T-shirt billowing, dipping around the curve, full of confidence, full of joy. I shoot across a low metal bridge, the trees close on the road again, and I disappear into a cathedral nave of limbs.

"You drive that thing?"

I have stopped at the Exxon station on the way home, and while the attendant pumps the combination of diesel and no-lead that I have requested, I submit to the skeptical scrutiny of the men in the car beside me.

"What is it?"

"A Stanley Steamer."

"What year is it?"

"Nineteen-oh-nine."

"How much is it worth?"

"Have to find someone who wants it first."

As I climb back into the driver's seat, my interrogator turns to his friend.

"I want to see her pull out," he says, from the Olympian heights of his male superiority.

I take off like a shot.

Home again, fuel valves closed, fires out, I open the blow-off valves beneath the front sill, and steam blasts forth, deafening, slightly shrill, in ever-expanding streams that extend a hundred feet in front of the car before evaporating. It is an awesome, almost incomprehensible, indication of the power contained in that machine and I am overcome with a sense of privilege that something so beautiful, so fine, its hidden power rendered so gentle, could be mine.

Sunday. One day until Bob Beck comes. I am still soaring after yesterday, the Stanley safe in the garage, the wind still in my ears. I am filled with George's pleasure, his pride in me. A peaceful Sunday. One more day.

Monday. Ed is cutting, hauling, filling.

Bob Beck calls. He's running late. He can't come. Can he come tomorrow? Or maybe Wednesday? I should have known this would happen. I'm so disappointed I'm not even very polite. I insist that he come tomorrow. He probably thinks I'm pretty rude. He's doing me a favor, after all. What if he's so offended he decides not to come at all? Would he do that? He's got to come. I simply can't cope if he doesn't. I didn't mean to be rude. What am I going to do if he doesn't? He's got to. One more day. He's just got to.

People dread writing letters of condolence, fearing the inadequacy of their words, the pain they must address, death itself. And few people realize, until the death of someone close, what a benediction those letters are.

The arrival of letters about George was a luminous moment of each day. They made me cry. They made me feel close to him. They gave me the sense that the love he inspired in others embraced me. The best were the longer, more specific ones, the ones that mentioned something the writer cherished in George, or recounted some tale from his past that I was unaware of. Others were inexpressibly poignant. At one time I would have avoided writing any such letter, thinking it unkind to dwell on a subject that was the source of such pain, that I would be rubbing salt into a wound. But now I know that it is not unkind. There is so much joy mixed in with the pain of remembering.

"My earliest memory of George was watching him *walk* up a stiff grade in Connecticut steering the Prescott from the side, and urging the little car to make the top, which it did."

"I'm glad I got a chance to tell him a few weeks ago that his selecting me to help him pack up the Hemingway and Fitzgerald files to send to Princeton was a turning point in my career—really!"

"Did he ever tell you how, day after day, he fouled up the machinery of woodcutters who were taking down chestnut trees on the property? He was about 15. Did he ever tell you that when subdividing the property in back of ours, he changed the route of the access road to save a red ash tree at my request? He was about 75."

"Had there been time he would have rid the world of pomposity, or at least made the pompous eternally miserable."

"He was never happier than he was with you."

"I know from experience how difficult this time is for you—part of you knew it wouldn't go on forever, but part of you believed it would. Now you're facing reality—and it hurts. And it will for a long time."

"Forgive me for not being at the funeral tomorrow. I wish I could, in that beautiful church, tell him thanks for all the dear things he has done for me. Tell him for me in your dear heart."

How I treasured those letters! All of them. I treasure them still. The problem was in answering them.

One of the few remaining things I could do for George was to try to ensure that everything associated with his death was fine. Part of my gift to him would be to reply fully to everyone who had made the gesture of writing. I would counter my grief with the thought that I was doing things well, as he would wish them done. But it was so difficult. I couldn't read the letters I had received without sobbing, much less frame a cogent sentence. I joked to a friend, "Brides are allowed a year to thank people for wedding presents. Couldn't I have a year to answer these letters?"

"Oh, no," she replied. "I think people expect to hear right away."

So I forged on, writing one, and later two or three, a day, to honor him.

Bob Beck is all eyes and smile, of medium height and build, one of those people who are bigger than the room they are in. Talking to him is a bit like talking to a beacon. He wears gray trail pants, with knit shirt and work boots, and when I tell him I am afraid of my house falling down, he laughs easily. But I know he understands that I am not really joking and that he will take my worries seriously.

I lead him up to the attic.

"You do have one problem," he says. "Your insulation has been installed upside down. In fact, it should have been put under the floorboards and not on the attic slopes. But regardless, it should be insulation side out. The way it is now, moisture is collecting and rotting the roof."

This seems an ominous beginning, but he seems so cheerful.

"I see you've had a fire." He has noticed the charred rafters in one section of roof.

"That's right. Ten or twelve years ago."

This seems not to concern him either. Nor does the fact that in one corner I can see daylight where the roof meets the floor.

In one of the guest rooms below, he eyes the sagging floorboards.

"The floor probably sags down to the ceiling underneath," he says.

I feel another wave of alarm.

"But that's okay."

He follows me through the rest of the house, examining windows, bathroom seals, ceilings, floors, walls. I show him where the rain has been coming in.

"The windows and the Dutch door just need caulking. You'll probably need new flashing where the kitchen roof meets the house to prevent the leaks in this doorway. A roofer will do that for you."

In the dark of the cellar, I am unable to suppress a shudder, in spite of the fact that I am not alone. I tighten the bulb in the ceiling fixture. It lights, and he turns slowly, scanning the walls.

"Good foundation," he says. I am touched. I feel sort of proud.

He flashes a light onto the circuit-breaker box.

"You have a hundred amps coming in," he says. "That means you have enough power for a clothes dryer, if you want to get one, and the electric stove, but you couldn't run them both at the same time."

"If I'm so low on power, that sounds like a good excuse not to cook."

He smiles at my outrageousness. He doesn't know that when I'm not in New York or invited out I eat lunch and dinner at the Spinning Wheel Diner.

He shines his flashlight upward. The moment of truth.

"You can see why they've added the Lally columns," he says. "Look at the distance the floor joists were being asked to support."

He runs his light along what I take to be the floor joists.

"And these beams run the entire width of the house," I observe.

"Girders," he corrects me. "Wood girders."

"Oh. Do you think they added the columns to keep the house from falling down?"

"Not really. More likely to keep the floor above from sagging any further. Your house is sounder than you think."

He doesn't think the house will fall down.

"You've got the same problem down here with the insulation, though."

Strips of insulation run parallel to the floor joists, paper side out.

"You'll have to remove this and put in new. I don't think you'll be able to reuse it."

Outside, he looks at roof, gutters, porch.

"Your foundation needs pointing up."

"What does that mean?"

"Do you see the spaces between the stones?"

"Yes."

"That's where the mortar has washed out."

"Doesn't that weaken the foundation?"

"In this case you have nothing to worry about. The stones haven't moved."

Good Lord. What's to keep them from moving to-morrow?

"I'll give you the name of a mason."

I ask him if the house will fall on the plumber when he's in the crawl space fixing the septic drain.

"No. Who is it? Fowler?"

"Yes."

"Then don't worry. Fowler knows what he's doing. He's not going to let a house fall on him."

Nonetheless, I find it all too easy to imagine the foundation stones next to the crawl space giving way, and the house crumbling, flattening the unsuspecting plumber.

"You might want to put on vinyl siding."

"Vinyl?"

"It's the most practical kind. Needs no upkeep."

"Maybe someday. For now I'd just like to be sure the house is sound."

"And if you extend the downspouts away from the house, you'll have less trouble with water in the cellar."

I scratch the names and phone numbers he gives me on several leaves of a small pad: carpenter—to reframe the porch roof, provide a new roof deck, shingles, and to replace random rotten boards in other parts of the house; roofer—to replace the flat roof over the kitchen and, if necessary, the roof on the main part of the house; gutter man; mason; insulation firm.

"You'll want to get whatever roof done before you do the gutters."

"Oh?"

I gather the slips of paper in my hands—the key to my salvation. How am I going to thank this man?

I suggest he send me a bill. Or would he like a ride in my Stanley Steamer? His eyes are as big as saucers.

"My kids would love it!" he exclaims. "That's a once-in-a-lifetime experience!"

Later, I discover that his children are girls, and I feel a new wave of warmth for this man who thinks to share something mechanical with his girls.

It's funny how much better you feel, just having set things in motion. The carpenter is coming in a couple of days to give me an estimate. The roofer and someone from the insulation company will be here next week. I've left a message on the gutter man's machine. The foundation man can't come for two or three months. But he promised he'd fit me in before it snows. Snows! I sure hope Bob is right about those stones.

I thought the plumber would send chimney sweeps! Instead he's sent two able-bodied, normal-sized men. They seem not the least appalled to discover that they can't get into the concrete-sealed, surely vermin-ridden crawl space from outside. The only access to the head of the broken section of septic drain is in the cellar, through a hole in the foundation. The hole is behind a network of pipes, rising out of the green cylindrical water pump that sits on a cinder-block column about a foot from the foundation wall. The hole is no more than six inches high and about three feet wide, and as they begin to remove foundation stones to enlarge it, I realize this is all I can bear to watch, and flee.

Upstairs, I hear their voices. From time to time, one of them scales the stairs, two at a time, and bounds out to their truck to get some piece of equipment, then returns downstairs. I straighten pictures, pick up specks of lint, open a can of food for Murray.

When they finish, they are still smiling. They show me, outside, the new brown plastic pipe, which they tell me will break less easily in cold weather. When they are gone, I return to the cellar with a flashlight. From the foot of the stairs, I can see that the foundation stones have been replaced. The drain has been fixed and the house hasn't fallen down. A velvet calm embraces me in the face of this miracle.

I woke up again in the middle of the night, feeling my way around the foot of the bed, having no idea where I was. That makes three times since the first time it happened. It hasn't been as terrifying these subsequent times, but still I have been alone, afraid, lost in the dark. You'd think that, by now, I would know where I am.

Grief intensifies all responses—to tragedy, to beauty, to the day-to-day. I watched nearly every televised moment of the Winter Olympics in Calgary, hanging on the pursuit of perfection, rejoicing in Brian Boitano, the men's figure-skating gold medalist, whose performance in the free skating pushed to perfection's outer limit. The images whirl in my mind: The smart set of the gold-braided shoulder. The triple Lutz under the arc of an upstretched arm. The wide, slow, backward cant of the spread eagle. His choreographer had told him, "It's your moment, show them your soul." And he had.

One man in tears of triumph, another in tears of loss. America's best hope for a gold medal in men's speed skating, Dan Jansen had talked to his sister by telephone on the morning of the 500-meter event. A brother had held a phone to her ear. She was suffering from leukemia. Three hours later she was dead. That evening, seconds into the 500, Jansen's skate slipped out from under him and he crashed into the side of the rink. On the following Thursday, he fell for a second time, nearing the finish of the 1,000. It was, as

Richard Lacayo wrote in *Time*, "as if he had been forced down by sorrow alone."

In the face of the exquisite, of death, of unbearable loss, one watches bemused and annoyed as the world hurtles by, getting and spending, oblivious to the essential cycle of life. Elbowed in the subway, obstructed by churlish store clerks, I wanted to cry out, "Can't you see my husband has died? Don't you care?"

I had no patience now with a lack of civility that I had heretofore taken for granted, even somewhat enjoyed. And I probably saw rudeness even where there was none. Helen Hayes spoke, after the death of her husband Charles MacArthur, of "taking umbrage at nothing at all."

The world intrudes in many small ways to underline one's grief. Only days after George died, a call came from Brooks Brothers, George's clothes were ready, should they send them? The sturdy blue boxes arrived, inside, a tweed jacket, in tan and forest green plaid; a navy blue blazer with gold Brooks buttons; gray flannel trousers; a three-piece suit in gray herringbone tweed; dinner clothes; all custom-made, ordered only weeks before. Soft, rich fabrics, finely cut, of no use now.

The fat manila envelope from the Funeral Directors lies on the doormat outside the front door. I know what is inside. George's lawyer has already telephoned to tell me that his set of Death Certificates has arrived. I put the envelope on a table, unopened, knowing I will not be able to bear the sight of George's name typed at the top of this official corroboration of his death. When, at last, I have the courage to look, I feel he has been sullied, his privacy invaded, by the uninterested hand of the City of New York.

The world at large does not guess at the pain inflicted by the small corroborations. After George died, while I was still living in the apartment, a friend called and exclaimed, "You've got to change the message on your answering machine! George is dead. It's GHOULISH to have his name on the tape! Yech!" How to explain that you cannot, yourself, erase this record of a moment in which he was alive, that you don't want it erased. That to erase it would be, again, to corroborate his death, to push him away. This is his home.

Barry Lopez wrote in *Harper's* of the dry valleys of Victoria Land in the Antarctic and the "scattering of mummified creatures on the valley floors, mostly young crabeater seals."

"No one is certain," he said, "why the seals come up here. A good guess is that they are inexperienced. But it is travel utterly in the wrong direction. They succumb eventually to starvation on these errant journeys. The wind freeze-dries their flesh. The faces, if they can be said to have an expression, are distraught, catatonic with a sudden, horrible misunderstanding of geography. They had made an error. Their lips were parted in some final incoherent noise. They had, most of them, died alone."

Distraught, catatonic, lips parted in some final, incoherent noise. In the expression of those seals I see the enormity of what has happened, to me, to Dan Jansen, to others. There is so much tragedy in the world. One has to ask how it is that we are expected to bear it.

"N o problem!"

Wayne, the carpenter, is here to give me an estimate for the new porch. Dressed in shorts, T-shirt, and hightop Reeboks, he brims with a muscular good health and good cheer that with his rich suntan and brush-cut blond hair make him a persuasive testimonial to the salubriousness of outdoor country life. He wears a cross on a chain around his neck. And he is *very young.*

He backs off the porch and onto the grass, notebook in hand, his eyes scanning the porch roof, then bounds back up the steps and walks the length of the porch, gazing at the peeling paint and the rotten boards overhead. With one foot on the railing, he grabs a porch post and swings himself up into a standing position, peering at the juncture of the post with the roof. He leans out, his back over the wisteria, the muscles of his neck stretched taut as he curves his body upward, as though he were chinning himself, to get a closer look, he tells me, at the layers of shingles on the porch roof, how the roof is flashed. Then he jumps down onto the concrete floor.

"No problem!" he says. "We'll pull off the shingles, and

the decking and the framing members. I think we can use the old posts. Then we'll run what's called a ledger board the length of the house and put up new rafters to abut the ledger board."

"Is that how it was done originally?"

"No. You see how the ends of these rafters go into the wall? That's how they're held in place. Our way is much more secure. We'll remove this row of sidewall shingles, and the wood siding underneath. Then we'll attach the ledger board to the studs."

"Studs?"

"Yeah."

I have no idea what studs are, but I hope I have them. I am too ashamed that my house may not be good enough to have studs to mention the possibility to Wayne.

"And we'll have to put the rafters closer together. The ones you have now are too far apart to support the weight of the roof—at least according to the building code."

Bob has told me this too. I just can't quite adjust to the fact that Wayne is *so young.*

"What kind of work do you usually do?" I inquire, chattily. I can't very well ask him if he's ever built a porch before.

"Oh, cabinetry, miscellaneous home carpentry. And lately we've been doing a lot of decks."

Presumably, mine is his first porch.

He pops his notebook shut. "Okay!" He is so buoyant. "Suppose I put some figures together and drop by tomorrow with an estimate? Will you be here?"

"I may not be, but you could slip it under the door."

"Great."

He reaches out to shake my hand, then heads for his car. He turns and waves. "Bye, Laurie."

And I thought it was going to be easy, now that I have all these names. But at my age anyone under thirty looks fifteen. I call Bob and he assures me that Wayne can do the job.

"But he's so young!"

"He worked with me for six years before starting out on his own. I promise you, he's okay."

I can't understand how someone who looks so young could have worked that many years for anyone.

"He said he's going to attach a board to the house to hold up the rafters."

"That's right."

"And he said what you said, that the rafters have to be closer together."

"He knows what he's doing."

Still, I'm in a quandary. I don't know anything about building a porch. I'm not qualified to make a judgment. What would George do? Would it be obvious to him that one shouldn't hire someone so young? Am I being irresponsible? I have a chance to put everything to rights. What if my very first move turns out to be a mistake? I want to think of the house as whole, sound, not harboring yet another flaw—especially one that I have introduced. Why in heaven's name have I allowed myself to live all this time without learning how to build a porch?!

Thank God for Ed. I see him through the kitchen window, approaching the house. He is wearing an aqua knit shirt and blue jeans, and after these days of watching him work he strikes me as the epitome of quiet competence. I step onto the porch to greet him. He looks up with a slightly sheepish smile as he wipes the beads of perspiration from his forehead.

"I guess that does it for now," he says.

We stroll around the house and grounds. The transformation is dramatic. The jungle look is gone. He has removed tree limbs that were scraping the porch roof and the lower limbs of the pines, the dead limbs of a maple tree; he has filled in the ditch, cut the shin-high grass to something approaching lawn length, filled in the holes, hauled off the remains of the fountain behind the house, leaving a patch of newly seeded earth, covered with straw. He has taken three feet from the sides and the top of the forsythia, six feet off of the holly tree.

"I took ten feet off that hedge!" He laughs.

The boxwood and the wisteria have been trimmed and he has taught me to weave the branches of wisteria back in upon themselves. Sometime in the next few weeks, he will seal off the cistern and build up the topsoil along the far side of the house. I have a long way to go, but the place is at least somewhat less the stuff of a Charles Addams cartoon.

"Should I try to get the foundation man here before you build up the soil?" I ask Ed.

"It doesn't really matter. He'll just remove what he needs to, and then put it back when he's finished."

"Okay."

We stop at the foot of the porch steps.

"How many loads of limbs and so on do you suppose you took out of here?"

"Well, let's see. The number 'thirteen' sticks in my mind. That means thirteen dump truck loads and thirteen pickup loads."

"How much does each truck hold?"

"Well, the bed of the dump truck measures eight feet long by six feet wide, and I figure each load was about nine feet high. The pickup bed measures eight feet long by five feet wide, and would have been piled about six feet high. Oh, and then there were six trailer loads. The trailer bed is sixteen feet long by eight feet wide, and the load must have measured about eight feet high. How much is that?"

"You've got me. How high are the sides of the trucks?"

"Two and a half feet."

"How could so much of the load extend above the sides?"

"We had it all tied down."

Later, I try to figure it out. The contents of the truck beds are easy enough—they're solid rectangles. I decide that for my purposes it will be enough to view the trailer loads and the part of the truckload that extends above the sides as trapezoids.

So. Eight feet long times six feet wide . . . an average of four and three quarters feet wide . . . 367 cubic feet . . . five feet wide, two and a half feet high . . . 212 cubic feet . . . sixteen feet . . . eight feet . . . a little over 742 cubic feet.

367 cubic feet times thirteen dump truck loads . . . 212 cubic feet times thirteen pickup loads . . . 742 cubic feet times six trailer loads. . . .

Ed has removed 11,979 cubic feet of vegetation, slightly more than the entire interior volume of the first and second stories of my house, minus the kitchen. A major part of it has come from within twenty to thirty feet of the house. It's no wonder that, at least in one respect, I feel like something that has crawled out from under a rock.

Bud tells me Wayne's estimate is fair. I still don't know what to do. I am so ill-equipped to decide, so afraid of making a mistake. I don't want to replace an old porch that will fall down with a new porch that will fall down. Everyone has to get his start somewhere. But why does it have to be with *my porch?*

Ah, the consolations of Art! I had asked three friends, "Have you seen the David Hockney show?" and three times received the same conversation-stopping reply, "I don't like Hockney very much." I am no expert on Hockney, but who could resist his sets for the Metropolitan Opera French triple bill called *Parade*—the naïvely rendered old port on the Riviera for Poulenc's *Les Mamelles de Tirésias,* the riot of line, the pulsing colors of the room, seen from the perspective of a child, in Ravel's *L'Enfant et les sortilèges.* In white safari shirt, khaki skirt, narrow tan linen necktie, I was Meryl Streep in *Out of Africa* this morning, as I made my way to the Hockney retrospective at the Metropolitan Museum.

One notices first in Hockney the quotations from other artists—the crude, sticklike figures of Jean Dubuffet, the modes of stylization in Picasso, the forms, the use of color, the dancers, even the goldfish bowl of Matisse—suffused in their new context with Hockney's gleeful wit. Even the titles make me smile: *Picture of a Still Life That Has an Elaborate Silver Frame; Religious Area with Equal Unreligious Area; A Man Stood in Front of His House with Rain Descending.*

One responds, even if only on the level of color and size, to the multifaceted view of *Mulholland Drive,* the seven-by-twenty-foot depiction from memory of the sweep of winding road, the shifting views, the variegated land patterns encountered on the drive from the artist's house in the Hollywood Hills to his studio in Santa Monica. One aches at the photocollage of his elderly mother, in blue-green hooded raincoat, black brogues, hunched on a gravestone at Bolton Abbey, in Yorkshire, eyes averted, uncomprehending, the polished tips of the artist's shoes in the foreground. One feels the rush of the desert wind on *Pearblossom Hwy.*—the receding succession of road signs, the shimmering collage propelling the viewer forward toward the vanishing point ahead on the horizon, while also offering other perspectives—the Joshua trees, the roadside litter, the road signs themselves.

Hockney works in a wide range of media and styles. He continues the cubist exploration of multiple perspectives, the incorporation by the Chinese scroll painter of the passage of time, of movement in time, of the observer, into the pictorial image. His art varies in manner and degree of abstraction. Hockney is a serious artist with serious concerns. But he seems, in large part, a cerebral one. Perhaps this is why my friends have said that they "don't like Hockney very much."

I lunch in princely solitude in the Doric-columned, grayed pink-walled dining room of the Met, on cold veal with pistachio sauce and a glass of white wine, then stop to call on two of my favorite paintings—*Saint Anthony Tempted by a Heap of Gold,* by the Master of the Osservanza, and Giovanni di Paolo's *The Creation, and The Expulsion of Adam and Eve from Paradise.* Both fifteenth-century Sienese. A long way from Hockney.

In the Osservanza Master, a robed and haloed Saint Anthony stands on a path in the foreground, hands lifted in surprise. (At what one could hardly know, without being told, as the heap of gold that has surprised him has since been scraped away and the area repainted.) Rising behind him is a foreshortened landscape of barren conical hills, a coral-colored abbey, twisted, arthritic trees, a greenish lake, and luminous clouds tinged rose by the sun just dipped below the horizon. The path on which he stands links the disparate areas of landscape and leads the eye in the top half of the painting toward a vanishing point on the horizon, yet in the lower half sweeps outward toward the viewer.

In the Giovanni di Paolo, a haloed, bearded figure of God, accompanied by blue, wingèd cherubim, descends from the upper left corner of the panel, his index finger on the rim of what resembles a giant wheel or plate, and is actually a symbolic, Dantesque rendering of the heavens and the earth. The earth is at the center, surrounded by color-coded rings of water, air, fire, the planets and the sun, the zodiac, and finally, the *primum mobile*, beyond which lies the measureless region of God. To the right of this image, an archangel forces Adam and Eve from Paradise. Largely because of His downward projection, one feels the energy of thunder in the figure of God, in the blue wings of the cherubim.

Home again, sitting on the porch steps, leafing through the Hockney catalogue, I am intrigued to find echoes of the Saint Anthony—the conical hill in *Mulholland Drive,* the winding path that links one disparate section to another, the symbolic landscape, the arthritic trees. In another Hock-

ney painting, *Nichols Canyon,* there is the same foreshorten-
ing, yet another winding path, receding to a vanishing point
in the hills of the horizon above, but as in the *Saint Anthony,*
widening, rushing toward the viewer at its base.

Hockney speaks in the catalogue of the connections
between his artistic concerns and modern physics, which has
broken down the Newtonian view of the universe as a machine that functions independent of man. Einstein's special
theory of relativity makes measurement relative to the observer, eliminating the objective, neutral viewpoint. Heisen-
berg's uncertainty principle shows the immeasurability, on
the subatomic level, of physical reality, the impossibility of
divorcing the effect of the observer from the measurement of
the observed. According to quantum mechanics, which is
based on the uncertainty principle, there can be no absolute
certainty, no one definite result for an observation, only a
range of possible results. Hockney points to the parallels in
art, in the concept of multiple perspectives, the interdepen-
dence of perspectives, which are central to the work of the
cubists. Man, the observer, has become part of the universe
again.

The celestial spheres of Dante, of Giovanni di Paolo,
seem quaint and charming to us now. But still we have no
final answers. Stephen Hawking writes in *A Brief History of
Time* that in order to arrive at a unified theory of the universe, we will have to find a new theory that will incorporate
general relativity (Einstein's extension of special relativity to
include the effects of gravity) and quantum mechanics. Only

when we have succeeded will we be equipped to address effectively, to achieve the resolution of, man's ultimate yearning—to find the reason for our existence, to "know the mind of God."

The place of my porch in the cosmos seems justly small now. The setting sun tinges the clouds here in north-central New Jersey. A lone jogger disappears behind a stand of trees. I'll go ahead with Wayne. Everybody has to start somewhere.

Part of me was slightly in awe of George. Even after we'd been seeing each other for months, he was still "Mr. Schieffelin" in my mind. Partly, no doubt, because he was my employer. And because he was part of a world that for most of us is out of reach. But partly, too, because there was a self-contained area, deep inside, that he did not share easily. And at the time, I wasn't yet aware of the lapses of confidence, the shyness, that resided in that private, independent core.

I remember vividly one of our first lunches together. It was a Saturday and he was wearing khaki-colored twill trousers and a jacket of hard-finished worsted, milled in Yorkshire, in a small gun club check of green, beige, black, highlighted by an occasional mustard pinstripe, and bone buttons. We were seated side-by-side on a banquette in a small Italian restaurant in the Fifties. The subdued lighting accented the planes of his face, the prominent brows, the graceful inward curve of his cheek, the oblique sweep of cheekbone toward his moonlit white hair. As he placed the tips of his fingers on the stem of his water glass, in what I would come to realize was a characteristic gesture, I caught sight of one of his gold cufflinks—rectangular, with a rounded edge, initials engraved in simple Roman capitals, the shiny surface muted, rubbed smooth by wear. I couldn't take my eyes off it, the warm, soft gold against the white cuff of his shirt. It was quiet, elegant, not meant to impress but simply a part of him, and it spoke volumes about who he was and where he had come from.

"I had to borrow a horse," he was saying, "and I thought I was so damned smart. A new Astor horse had just been delivered to the stable. I knew Astor wouldn't be out, and I thought I was clever as hell to have gotten the horse before anyone else. What I didn't know is that he was a former racehorse who had never been in the hunting field. I couldn't hold him for nuts. He wasn't about to have anyone ahead of him. I outran the entire field. My mother was ready to kill me." He chuckled, pushing his shoulders into the back of the banquette, arm extended forward on the table, his smile lingering at the memory of his having outsmarted himself and of his mother's wrath at his unspeakable infraction of fox-hunting etiquette.

After we had been seeing each other for a while, I developed an insistent ache, about the diameter of an apple, over my heart. I could make the pain go away temporarily, when we were together, by pressing that area of my chest against his shoulder, bare skin against bare skin. We slept like spoons. Or, rather, he slept. I lay awake, or dozed lightly, not wanting to miss a moment of his presence, my love for him swelling, spreading against his warm, soft skin. By morning, the yearning ache would be soothed. But, once he was gone, the unguarded edges of my need for him would surface again, and I would feel again the pain of fullness and longing.

After George died I left everything in the apartment as it was, his pipes atop a nest of tables in the living room, the shirts and trousers laid across a chair in the bedroom, the pairs of shoes lined up underneath. I would pause, often, as I passed by his mahogany bureau, my eyes caressing the vestiges of his life—the pile of pocket change, the laundry and dry-cleaning tickets, the American Express receipts, the unanswered letters, keys, the brass fittings from an old family table, his cufflinks. Our cleaning woman, who had worked for the family for years, offered to clear his toilet articles from the bathroom. I begged her not to. When she moved his shoes to the closet, I brought them out again, lined them up under the chair.

At night I would lie on my side of the bed, never straying to his, except from time to time to lay my hand, flat, against the pristine surface of the bedclothes, as though to touch whatever of him remained there.

In time, when I became more able to dispose of his things, it was in part because I had decided to keep what I most treasured—the jacket he had worn that day in the restaurant, his black hunting coat, the shirt and trousers he had worn to the hospital, his blue overcoat. They hang in my closet now. And on a shelf in the bathroom, a small black can of Tabac shaving foam, a tube of Meltonian shoe cream, a graduated medicine glass, a nail brush, his hair brush, a prescription box of nitroglycerin patches. In the drawer of my bed table, his gold cufflinks.

In the top drawer of the bureau I left an undershirt, shorts, a pair of socks, a clean shirt, neckties, muffler, gloves. They are still there. Everything he might need.

Gray fog squats behind a veil of falling rain. The air is heavy, water pools in my driveway. And Lewis has just arrived with the electrician. It seems, meteorologically speaking, a most inauspicious moment to be messing around with wires, but I put on the jacket of my L. L. Bean rain suit and lead the two men to the spot where I have placed the large, flat rock.

"It's not a very nice day to be working," I say to the electrician. His name is Ekstrom.

"Can't stop because of a little rain," he tells me, cheerfully. "And at least it's cooled off some."

Everyone here is so cheerful.

"The wire is under this rock."

Lowering himself onto one knee, he lifts the rock to reveal what he identifies as the three segments of a direct burial wire, three sections of No. 14 wire wrapped to size 3. He pulls his wire cutters out of his back pocket and fits the short, curved blades around the first segment. My heart skips a beat, as I have never seen anyone electrocuted before, and it seems altogether possible that the opportunity is at hand. After the muffled snap of the first cut, he is still alive. He fits the blades around the second segment, and cuts. Then the third. Still, he is alive. This seems to me an extraordinary piece of luck. He places one of the leads of his voltage meter against one clipped end of wiring, then another. His practiced hands move astonishingly quickly.

"They're dead," he concludes, unconcerned.

I am not sure that he has tested one of the ends, but there is something in me that doesn't want to challenge his conclusion.

"This is his profession," I tell myself. "Just trust him."

But when they leave I replace the rock.

I can't get rid of my doubts. Once the rain has stopped, I go to the hardware store and ask for one of those things you use to test whether wires are alive or not.

"You mean a Detecto-Lite?"

"I don't know. I guess so."

The Detecto-Lite consists of a translucent red plastic head, with light bulb, and two test prongs. It comes stapled to a piece of cardboard that reads: "Excellent for testing household appliances; switches, receptacles; lines & polarity; spark plugs; fuses; motors; grounded wires; and for making hundreds of other electrical tests." I feel foolish asking the clerk if it will work on wires coming out of the ground, so I decide to hope that wires coming out of the ground fall into the category of "hundreds of other electrical tests."

Presumably, if the wires are alive, the bulb in the red plastic head will light when I touch them with one of the prongs.

"You may regret this," I tell myself as I lift the rock off the wires. "If you live to know the difference."

I touch a prong to one of the wire ends. No light. I touch it to a second. No light. A third. No light. A fourth. A fifth. The sixth. I touch the wire ends with the other prong. With both prongs at the same time. No light.

I am relieved. But still, I cover the wires again with the rock.

"Bob always calls me for the tough ones." Mike Kravik smiles, shading his eyes with his hand as he squints upward toward my roof. He is a rough-hewn, country man, bald but for the exuberant sideburns and the fringe of graying black hair at the base of his skull. He is in blue jeans and a mustard-colored canvas shirt, which he wears unbuttoned, like a jacket, over his white T-shirt.

"Do I need a new roof on the main part of the house or just on the kitchen?"

"You need both," he says. "The shingles up top are totaled. They're all blistered and cracked."

"Will you have to take them off?"

"Oh, yeah."

"Then what?"

"We nail the decking tight. Then we install felt tar paper, and the edging. Then the new shingles."

"How do you attach the tar paper? With nails?"

"That's right."

"And the shingles?"

"Four nails per shingle. The shingles are self-sealing too."

He tells me about the frustrations of his work.

"People take their roofs for granted," he says. "A roof isn't glamorous like butcher block counter tops or sunken bathtubs. And they start yelling if they think the price is too high."

He kicks at something in the grass.

"But they don't think about my costs. You'd be amazed how much I have to figure in just to dispose of the old roof."

He shakes his head in exasperation.

"I was giving a quote on a $35,000 slate roof the other day and the guy wanted a break on the price!"

He places one hand on the fender of his truck, the other on his hip.

"If he can afford slate, he can afford to pay for it."

"You'd certainly think so."

"But, what're you gonna do. I like being outdoors. I like the work."

At the dining room table, he writes up an estimate. For the flat roof of the kitchen: Install Nord Bitumi single-ply roofing system; new flashings; new aluminum cap on walls; coat with aluminum fibrated roof coating. For the steep, gabled roof of the main part of the house: Remove 2 layers of shingles; install No. 15 pound felt tar paper; install new aluminum roof edging; install new flashings—pipes— chimney—etc.; install GAF 25-year self-sealing fiberglass shingles; remove all debris; 15-year workmanship guarantee; 25-year material guarantee. The price is almost exactly what Bob has told me it would be.

"If you decide to go ahead, I can be here in about a month."

After he leaves, I look at the estimate again, each item carefully set out, in the lower left corner, his signature— Thank you. Mike Kravik.

I'll be going to New York tomorrow. I back my VW Rabbit to the oblong silver gasoline tank next to the garage, remove the gas cap from the car, and splash some gasoline onto the blacktop to get rid of any insects that might have secreted themselves in the hose, and might otherwise find their way into the bowels of my car. I place the hose nozzle into the filler neck and turn back to rotate the pump handle when my eye catches the dark, oozing area of blacktop where for six years I have presumably been directing my initiatory splashes of gasoline.

I've never noticed it before! What if it catches on fire?!

I finish pumping gas into the Rabbit, then search the garage for some sort of tool. I decide on a crowbar, and some paper towels. On my knees, I chisel at the blacktop, strain against it, digging deeper, wider, blotting the oozing surface with paper towel. Chisel, blot, chisel, blot. The gasoline evaporates. The surface dries. I dig again. Only to find more ooze. I sweep the excavated blacktop, dry now with exposure to the air, into an ever-enlarging mound. I'll never get all this up!

I call Lewis.

"Nah, that's nothing to worry about," he says. "Someone would have to shoot a spark or flame right at it to start a fire. And it evaporates so fast."

I return, with a four-gallon-size Glad bag, to the blacktop, the hole, the pile of tar-covered pebbles, the mass of black-flecked, gasoline-stained paper towels that I have secured with the crowbar. With the paper towels, I sweep the loose blacktop into the plastic bag and back off, doubtfully. I am not confident there is no danger of fire, but there is a limit to how far I can dig. I return the crowbar to the garage and carry my bag of paper towels and blacktop to the house, where, for safety's sake, I set it in one of the rectangular basins of my double kitchen sink. At intervals, throughout the afternoon, I go back to the garage, to make sure there is no fire.

But where do I leave the bag when I go to bed? It's safe enough in the kitchen, I tell myself. The sink is part of an unvarnished counter, stained in a dull, medium brown, that juts into the center of the room. The plastic of the counter top doesn't look inflammable. I move the box of coffee filters to the table below. But what if it starts to smolder? The kitchen is so far from my bedroom, the flames could reach the ceiling before I even woke up. Could it start smoldering? It's really not wet anymore. Is the odor of gasoline inflammable? I try to remember what my elementary school teacher told me about spontaneous combustion.

I pluck the bag out of the sink and in my nightgown climb the stairs in search of a fireproof spot closer by. Metal waste basket? The linoleum floor of the upstairs bathroom? I settle on the bathtub. I take the (inflammable) towels from the bathtub rack and pull the rug away from the tub, then remove it from the bathroom altogether. Then I crawl into bed, hopefully eyeing the cheerful red fire extinguisher by the closet, the smoke detector, my first purchase for the house after George died, over the bedroom door.

I can't go to town and just leave it! And the garbage pickup isn't until Thursday. If I'm even allowed to put it out for them. Is this hazardous waste? We aren't supposed to leave hazardous waste. I could hide it in my other garbage. But what if their truck caught on fire, or something?

I look down at the white plastic bag in my bathtub. It still smells, faintly, of gasoline. My rational self tells me I am being ridiculous. "But," I say aloud, "if you really think you can't leave it, you'll just have to take it with you."

I open the trunk of the Rabbit. No. If it starts to burn on the way into town, I won't know until too late. I put the bag on the floor of the back seat. I will throw it away in New York.

I exit the Lincoln Tunnel and head up Tenth Avenue, scouting garbage cans. It's a bright, sunny day. The choice of can is important—it must be far enough away from any buildings and it must be located at a busy corner. That way, if the bag starts to smolder, someone will see it and put the fire out.

I lurch up the west side of Tenth Avenue, speeding, slowing, sizing up one can, then another, till I find the ideal—building set back, lots of pedestrians. I ignore their bemused, sometimes hostile stares as I climb out of the car, open the door to the back, take hold of the plastic bag, and deposit it in the garbage can. Then, head high, breathing a sigh of relief, I get back into the car and pull out into traffic, ready to begin my day.

George thought the way to get through life was to make a game of it. He viewed the human comedy unfolding around him as a vast entertainment, seldom judging but simply observing, rejoicing in people's strengths, amused by their foibles. With a gleam in his eye, he would stand at a party, feet firmly planted, hands in his pockets, watching— people on the make, people trying to impress one another, the budding romance, the undercurrents, the small maneuvers others didn't see. There was an underside—when he felt threatened, as he did sometimes in the context of his own social milieu, he could lash out. But that was not the essential George.

He reveled in his world at Scribners—the office intrigues, the interplay of personalities, the distinguished editor, so formal that (his wife was known to joke) his one sartorial concession on going to the beach was to wear tennis shoes with his navy blue suit. This same editor won the turkey draw at a pre-Christmas party at the New Jersey house, and George was jubilant at reports of him later at the station, cozying up to one trash can, then another, almost succeeding in losing the beast, before one of his colleagues would catch him in the act.

He accepted people for what they were. When notified by the police, yet again, that one of his best salesmen had been on a bender, winding up in the drunk tank, disheveled, wallet stolen, George flew out to see him, got him cleaned up, bought him a new suit of clothes, another new wallet, set him on his feet so that he could get back to work. He was simply an employer, who had, every year or so, to help an employee out of a moment of weakness.

He was generous, too, in a more literal sense. And these acts of generosity, too, became a game. One of the assistant editors, who had resigned her position at Scribners, was to leave the following day for a trip to London before starting her new job at another publishing house. In the interoffice mail that morning came a copy of the arts section of the London *Times*, with a five-pound note slipped into the theater listings, a farewell gift from George.

One evening he arrived at my apartment with a *Nuremberg Chronicle* in a brown paper bag. He said nothing, simply took it out of the bag and put it on the coffee table. At nineteen inches long, thirteen inches wide, and three and a half inches thick, weighing sixteen pounds, it was hard to miss.

"What's this?" I asked.

"One of the first best sellers."

The *Nuremberg Chronicle* was printed in 1493. Illustrated with woodcuts by Dürer's former master Michael Wolgemut, it is a history of the world from the creation to the present (1493), with a look ahead to the coming of the Anti-Christ, the final battle of the Heavenly Host with the armies of Satan, and the Day of the Last Judgment. The copy on my table was bound in blind-tooled pigskin over wooden boards. It was part of his collection of early German books.

"I'd like you to have it," he said. "You're the kind of person who would appreciate it."

It wasn't my birthday, or Christmas. He had simply decided to give it to me.

On the day of our wedding, he said to the clergyman, "I gave the preacher twenty bucks at my first wedding. I don't see why I should pay any more for this one."

He reached into his pocket and pulled out a small leather pouch. Inside was a twenty-dollar gold piece, worth about $600 at the time.

One year, shortly before Christmas, George sent a chair around to the home of his cousin Charlie Scribner. It made its entrance, shrouded in packing material, and with its low, blood-red velvet seat, the cabriole legs, and the sober, disproportionately tall and narrow banister back, seemed hardly more alluring once the shroud had been removed.

"George usually sends wonderful presents," Joan Scribner exclaimed. "But this year he's really sent a lemon!"

One could only wonder why George had sent this unusual-looking chair, surely not the Chippendale or Hepplewhite that one is accustomed to. It wasn't as if the Scribners were short of chairs.

"Thank you for the handsome present," Charlie said, somewhat wanly, on seeing George at the office the following morning.

George sensed a certain lack of enthusiasm.

"Did you take a good look at that chair?"

"Well, yes."

"You go home and have a good look at that chair."

That evening, Charlie pulled the chair out of the closet and examined it, at last finding the plaque giving its provenance. The chair had belonged to Isaac Newton. One of Charlie's heroes in the history of science. And justly so. Stephen Hawking points out that for all the greater precision of Einstein's general relativity, it is Newton's theory of gravity that, for all practical purposes, we use. For Charlie, the chair is a physical link to this genius who has so informed his life.

A couple of years after we were married, George came to me and said, "We're going to Somerville."

It was a quiet Saturday in the country. I had no desire to go to Somerville. But I kept my mouth shut. Twenty minutes later he pulled up in front of the New Jersey Division of Motor Vehicles.

"You got a dollar on you?" he asked.

"Yes."

He waited while I pulled my wallet from my bag, took out a dollar, and offered it to him.

"You hold on to it for now."

He got out of the car and went inside. I followed.

He was about to transfer the title to the Stanley Steamer to me. He was going to sell it to me for a dollar.

He understood how the world worked. We hired two horses one Saturday at a clean but rundown stable in

Vermont. Our guide was the daughter of the owner, about thirteen, impeccably polite, with the natural reserve of the New Englander. She deserved more from life than she seemed likely to get. On our return, George asked how much he owed her.

"That will be fourteen dollars."

He rummaged through his pockets, through handfuls of rumpled bills, unable for the moment to find what he was looking for. When, finally, he succeeded, he counted out fourteen dollars, a ten and four ones, and handed them to her.

"Thank you very much."

Then he handed her another ten. Caught unawares, she was unable to prevent the surge of pleasure from showing, however briefly, before drawing her dignity, like a curtain, back across her face.

"You had lots of twenties," I said to him later. "Why didn't you just give her a twenty and four ones?"

"There's something you haven't thought of," he said.

"What?"

"This way, she can decide for herself whether she wants to give her father the other ten."

He wasn't above a prank. When some printing plates were damaged in storage because they hadn't been packed with enough straw, George protested, but the storage firm refused to accept responsibility. It wasn't their fault if Scribners hadn't ordered enough straw. A few weeks later, the president of the storage company was dining with his wife at the Plaza. As the waiter removed the soup plates, two stevedore types thumped into the dining room and heaved a bale of straw onto the table. George had made his point.

Franklyn L. Rodgers, who was eventually to become president of Scribners, was in his final interview before joining the firm. George asked him, "Do you have a good voice?"

"Well, I do actually," Lee replied. "And I've had some experience. I've done some choral singing."

"Good. We have a carol sing in Rockefeller Center with Simon & Schuster each year at Christmas. We'll want you to try out."

"I will," Lee assured him.

Months went by, Christmas was approaching, and still Lee had received no notice of a tryout. Finally, it came to him. A *carol sing?!* With *Simon & Schuster?!* This was just George having fun. There was no carol sing.

At least I could understand the insulation man. He was here yesterday, a trim young man, in shirt and tie, making notes on a clipboard. He will blow in six inches of new insulation under the attic floor, and install 6-inch R-19 kraft-faced fiberglass insulation in the cellar. The old insulation will be disposed of. He will schedule the job for October 11th, when the new roof will surely have been completed.

The gutter man may as well be speaking another language. I can't even take hold of the words. A tall, slender man, as long and thin as one of his seamless gutters, he tries to explain what he can do himself and what has to be done by somebody else. But the glare of the sun as I squint upward distances me from the words I feel I have never heard before. Faced with my continued incomprehension, he gives up. He will sort it out with Bob and the roofer and tell me how they decide to proceed.

George loved women—the soft contour of a cheek or a breast, the elegant line of a Lanvin gown, the lush aura of the feminine Other. And he liked women competent.

One of his ideals—the gentle-born Hannah Lawrence, who to the dismay of her rich and proper Quaker parents, and in spite of her own pro-colonial sympathies, eloped in 1780 with the handsome Jacob Schieffelin, a British Army officer, who had been quartered in her family's house during the British occupation of New York, and whom she had known for only two months. They spent a first, rugged and snow-ridden, winter in the wilds of Fort Niagara, where she proved more than equal to being seated at a campfire, under the protection of an inverted canoe, at the side of her Indian host, who had a Yankee scalp dangling from his ear. When the war was over, it was her poem lampooning the strutting

British occupation force, which she had had privately printed in 1779 and had dropped on the ground for the British officers to find, that most eased their entry into the life of the new American nation.

And there was Tempe Wick, set upon, as legend has it, in 1780 near Washington's encampment in Morristown, New Jersey, by soldiers in need of horses. They ordered her to dismount. She chatted charmingly, threw them off their guard, then touched her horse with her whip and took off amidst a hail of bullets. Reaching her house, she sprang down, and led the horse through the kitchen and the parlor to the guest room, where she kept him for three weeks. When the troops moved on, the horse was free to take up residence again in the barn.

Being part of a family with no ear for music, George mistakenly assumed that I couldn't sing either.

"You think I can't sing?!" I exclaimed. "Come with me."

I led him into the study, where I put on a recording of a small singing group I had belonged to at school. He listened, with tears in his eyes, at the sound of eleven young female voices in song.

The pulse of rock music from Wayne's radio and the steady twang of an electric saw provide the aural backdrop for the dismantling of my porch. Wayne and Paul, his partner, move deftly over the porch roof, their robust and youthful good looks in stark contrast to the decay of my prematurely agèd house. Their surefootedness and economy of movement bespeak a competence that underscores the disproportion of my churning anxiety about Wayne's age. Already they have removed the shingles, which now lie in a pile by the driveway.

"The porch had three roofs, Laurie," Wayne calls down to me.

Three layers of shingles, that is, one more than the two allowed by the building code. I take hold of a piece of the roof deck which has caught in the wisteria. It is spongy, wet with rot. It gives softly as I squeeze. This is what has been overhead. I wonder at Wayne and Paul's safety. But they know what they are doing.

George was sensitive, too, to courage and achievement. He would swallow a sob, as Charles Lindbergh, in the film version of *The Spirit of St. Louis,* landed at Le Bourget to the roar of the Paris crowd. He relished the memory of running into Lindbergh at the elevator, late one evening, on the editorial floor of the Scribner Building. The weather was frigid and George was wrapped in heavy overcoat, hat, scarf, gloves. Lindbergh, who had been reading proofs, wore only a business suit.

"It's cold out there," George warned, his eye on Lindbergh's suit.

"Not at all," Lindbergh replied. "You forget I'm from Minnesota!"

He spoke less often of certain private memories of Scribner authors. It is a friend who tells of George's thoughts on Thomas Wolfe, as he expressed them to her, with a lyricism that was not characteristic.

"Many people found Wolfe completely unmanageable," he said. "I found him the most humane of Scribners' authors, my favorite. I had the privilege of knowing him outside the literary tangles. He was an exquisite man, an eloquent man, a man who not only had the courage to live life, but who felt it acutely.

"We got on very well, Wolfe and I. It may have been our sense of humor that brought us together. I don't know. But one thing I do know is that no one could express himself as Wolfe did. He would casually voice an idea or a perception and it was as though a shaft of morning light had entered the room. A tenderness would settle in. And then he would be done with it. I loved him."

"**I**'d like to stop by this afternoon with some samples," Mike Kravik tells me by telephone. "You'll want to pick out a color."

"Color?"

Until this moment it hasn't occurred to me that roofs come in colors. Roofs are black.

On the way to lunch I survey the roofs along the route to the diner. I am astonished. There are brown ones, beige ones, light gray, dark gray, pale green, deep green, deep rusty red. There are chiaroscuros of one hue, of black-mottled green, gray-mottled blue. There is brown, with rectangles of mustard. And there is black. Mike Kravik is right at least where I am concerned. I have certainly never given much thought to my roof.

A postal reminder from the county Health Department: "What you are putting down your drains may very well come out of your faucets in the months ahead."

"Bad news, Laurie."

The posts have been removed, along with the roof deck and frame, leaving only the naked block railing and the concrete floor of my porch.

"The posts turned out to be rotten at the base and they're

full of carpenter ants. I'm afraid you're going to have to get new ones."

The posts have been tossed onto the lawn, from where they stood. Alone in the grass, they have the look of soldiers that have been betrayed.

"I guess it can't be helped."

Along the former roof line, I catch sight of what must be the ledger board. I wonder if this means that I do indeed have studs.

"Is that the ledger board?"

"Yes, it is."

"It's attached to the studs?"

"That's right."

I laugh. "I was afraid my house was so crummy it might not have studs."

"Nah. You not only have studs, but they're real two-by-fours."

"What does that mean?"

"Two-by-fours don't measure two by four anymore. What's called a two-by-four nowadays is actually one and five-eighths by three and five-eighths."

"Why is that?"

"A combination of reasons. They used to be cut from old-growth lumber that didn't shrink as much as the fast-growth pine we use now. And the old two-by-four was rough-hewn. Now they're rough-hewn and dressed down to a smaller size. They're also cut a little less than to size to begin with."

So my house has real two-by-fours. Again, I feel a touch of pride.

Paul and Wayne have come in separate trucks, and after Wayne leaves, Paul remains behind. The air is pleasant and we stand together in the gentle, evening sun. Paul's face is fine-boned, and his blunt-cut blond hair, cut short along the part line, falls forward over one eye and brushes his collar at the back. There is something self-contained about him, a calm that suggests a wisdom and perspective unusual in someone so young. He tells me that he once started the Great American Novel, but had decided his work didn't measure up and had quit. In the garage, he looks with quiet and lingering appreciation at the cars. He seems happy. But it is difficult not to feel that, in this small community, something is going to waste.

The telephone rings.

"Hello?"

"Is Mr. Schieffelin there?"

"Who's calling?"

"Bill Tanner from L.A."

"I'm afraid Mr. Schieffelin died in January."

Click.

For about a month after George died I woke up gasping. The pain would catch me each morning almost by surprise, and, lying on my side, I would clutch my pillow against the obdurate bulge in my chest. Finally, it would burst out of me and I would sob helplessly until I could get out of bed and walk.

Once the family had left and I had settled into a routine, the pain followed a daily cycle, slowly dissipating after the awful moment of awakening, until by evening I often felt "just fine," "over it." I would sit in front of the television, exhausted, but a little cocky with my recovery. Then morning would come again and with it the pain that left me gasping.

After that, the morning anguish turned to fear. For months I woke up terrified. I still do.

"You're starting a whole new life," friends say. "And you have to decide what it's to be. Of course you're terrified."

"You're alone in the country, someone might break in. No wonder you're scared."

But I know that's not why I'm frightened. I try to think of something concrete that I am afraid of and I can't. The house is under control. For the moment, I choose to be alone. And once I get up, I am no longer so afraid. But still each morning, before five o'clock, I awaken in the dark, clutching my pillow, wanting to cry out into what remains of the night.

I'm beginning to get a handle on gutters. Bob Beck called. Mike Kravik will install new drains in the wooden gutters, to channel water to the downspouts, and the gutter man will extend the downspouts away from the foundation, and install aluminum gutters along the porch and along the window side of the kitchen. I wonder why I couldn't understand that before.

The porch is taking shape. The header sits on top of the new posts and the rafters have been nailed secure to the ledger board. Next come the plywood sheets that will make up the roof deck.

"When is the painter coming?" Wayne asks me.

Until this moment, it hasn't occurred to me that I'll need a painter.

"I have a friend who can probably come right away," he says. "You'll at least want to get all this primed before it rains."

"He's a good painter?"

"Oh, yeah. He does a lot of work for me."

I suggest he call his friend, and with the porch nearing

completion, ask if he will install new exterior casing around the doors and the worst of the windows (casing being the correct term for what I have been calling a frame), order new screen doors, caulk the window and the Dutch door in the kitchen, and make a new storm window, and cover a hole to nowhere under the kitchen sink. Now that I've got him, I'm not going to let him get away.

Six months license suspension, $250 to $500 fine, insurance surcharge of $1000 a year for three years. Right? Wrong. That's for refusing to take a breath test. Then what's driving while intoxicated? $250 to $400 fine, possible imprisonment for thirty days, loss of license for six months to a year. How are you supposed to remember which is $250 to $400 and which is $250 to $500? Driving with a suspended license. $500 fine and up to six months additional license suspension. Then what's the $1000 fine for? Altering a driver's license.

I've had four driver's licenses in my life. And after the first one I certainly didn't study. But they're serious here. You should see the sample test!

How long do you have to notify the DMV of an address change? One week. Of a name change? Two weeks. Or is it two weeks for an address change and one week for a name change? Why are they different? You have to get an 80 to pass. What if I flunk? Forged or counterfeit license plates. Up to $500 fine, up to sixty days in jail. Driving an uninsured vehicle . . .

August 23rd. I have to deliver my water sample by ten o'clock. I turn on the tap in the kitchen, and place the plastic sample cup, in its sealed plastic bag, and the instructions for tap water sampling on the counter to my right. *Do not take the sample from a faucet that leaks around its stem, or from a faucet that contains an aeration device or screen within the faucet.* I have screens in all my faucets, but Lewis has removed the one in the kitchen. None of my faucets leaks around its stem. *Let the water run to waste for at least 5 minutes.* I look at my watch. 8:36. *Keep the sample cup unopened until the moment it is to be filled.* 8:41. I take the sample cup, tear off the plastic wrapping. *Remove the cap, keeping fingers off the inner surfaces of the lid and cup, and out of the water collected. Hold the sample cup upright near the base while it is being filled.* I gasp as the cup bobbles slightly. *Avoid splashing. Do NOT rinse the cup with the sample. Fill it directly to the brim.* I shut off the tap. The water quivers at the top of the cup. *Asceptically replace the cap, making sure it is tight.* I push down on the cap. The cup gives alarmingly. I am a little nervous. I write my name and the date on the label provided and drive to the Municipal Building, sample in lifted hand, as if it were as valuable as diamonds.

I got a hundred on my driver's test. And I didn't even have to know that stuff about drunken driving.

Comfort comes from unexpected sources after a death, slips in quietly, providing moments of beneficent calm in the wracking sea of pain. In the weeks after George died, I would sit in the apartment, in a chintz-covered armchair, my eyes resting on the windows at the far end of the living room, the sunlight muted by the airy, nearly translucent fabric of the Austrian shades. And I would think what so many others had thought before me.

"I have no place in the world." I knew now what that meant. I, too, had lost my sense of place, the sense that I had a right to be in the world. Not because I derived my identity from my husband, but because he and I were one.

I understood what people meant when they said, "My time has come." The structure of my life had fallen away. I identified with the generation that was passing and not with the one to which I belonged. My own death, were it to come soon, would be natural, appropriate. But far from being unpleasant, for me these thoughts were a source of peace. In witnessing the process of death, I had come, for the moment, not to fear it, but to see it as the culmination of life. "Because I could not stop for Death, / He kindly stopped for me." And George's death had been, in sum, a gentle one.

My pain, too, became a source of comfort. It meant that George was present. I came to dread its fading. Once it was gone, I would have lost him.

On my rides I listen to country music. It is good driving music. And however sentimental, it speaks, simply, to what is elementally human. "Could I have this dance for the rest of my life? / Would you be my partner ev'ry night?" Anne Murray. "If we never meet again this side of Heaven / I'll leave this world loving you." Ricky Van Shelton.

It is a cry from the heart. And it says some of what I want George to know.

I have been exploring my house, mentally peeling back the layers of improvements to determine its original configuration. The first determination was easy. As the toilet flushed in the upstairs bathroom, I heard water spilling down pipes, encased in floor-to-ceiling boards, in the corner of the hallway by my double front doors. The downstairs bathroom occupies an area that was once part of the sewing room. Wainscoting lines three of the sewing room walls. The newer, fourth, wall cuts too close to the window for symmetry. The tiny bathroom is on the other side. A friend tells me it is not surprising that the house was built without bathrooms. There was no electricity here either before the late twenties or early thirties. I show her a chimney that bears no relation to my furnace chimney. It begins in the living room and continues upward through a guest room closet. A rectangular cut remains in the boards of the attic floor.

"Don't kid yourself," she says. "Before the coal furnace, the house was heated by stoves."

The appraiser has indicated that the kitchen is a later addition. Which room, I wonder, was the kitchen before? The room we used as a dining room, with its door to the outside? Or was it the sewing room, with its wainscoting? There is wainscoting in the kitchen I have now. And it is just behind the sewing room that Ed found the cistern.

I stroll around the outside of the house. One of the asbestos shingles has come loose. Underneath I can see the dirty gray of the formerly white wood siding. Asbestos shingles would have been regarded in the forties as a great step forward, something new in a place where the old had no charm. Everything here was old. Asbestos shingles needed little upkeep. They were fireproof, and they provided additional insulation. To my eyes they are also ugly.

At the front of the house I look carefully at the façade. For the first time I notice the wooden cornices over the windows. Faded green and cracked, but still imparting a dignity unexpected of my house. I retrieve a snapshot of the old porch, taken before Wayne dismantled it. The sawtooth ornamentation on the gable over the doors is surely incompatible with the classic elegance of the cornices. And Ed tells me that contoured block was particularly popular here in the forties.

Was the porch a replacement of an original, wooden, porch? Added when the asbestos shingles were added, and with much the same end in view? The concrete and the contoured blocks would have required little upkeep.

My house stands before me in my imagination, trim white clapboard, cornices over the windows, porch rail and floor made of wood. There is no single-story box at the rear. The cistern behind the kitchen is filled with water. An outhouse stands behind a shrub. Simpler times.

What is going on?! I lift my head from the pillow to see the floor lamp teeter toward the window, then rock back onto its base. Mariah's saucer of cat chow has been overturned. The rug lies in unpressed accordion pleats against the massive footpost of my bed. Murray flashes across the room and lands with a thud against the closet door. Something chirps.

"Oh, boy," I say aloud, lying back onto the pillow. "Our first mouse."

I close my eyes and listen for a moment to the continued thrashing and banging, then rise onto one elbow as the round gray mouse scuttles the length of the room and wraps himself into a tight little ball among the coils of the radiator. Murray trots after him, settling himself companionably alongside, his big front paws curled into the white bib of his chest. I guess this is the end of my nap.

Eleven P.M. Catching Murray off guard, the mouse bursts from the ungiving metal coils of the radiator and swoops under the closet door into the sprawl of footgear and miscellaneous paraphernalia that lines my closet floor. I picture him hunched in the toe of one of my shoes. Murray is too wise to risk the indignity of lumbering through the clutter, and stations himself by the door. I think he is smiling. I move my new Armani suit to the bathroom in anticipation of the mayhem to come.

Three A.M. Here we go. The mouse squeaks. Squirms out of Murray's grasp. Murray thumps after him, pounces. The mouse is pinned again, lets out a long, pitiable squeal. I tell myself they are simply acting out the predator-prey relationship. It doesn't help. I don't want to be attendant at the dismembering of this fat little mouse. It escapes again. I lie flat, imagining the horror of lowering myself to the floor, bare feet landing on its gray velvet back, or worse, feeling the prickle of its toenails as it scrambles over my toes.

All becomes quiet. Cowardice gets the better of me and, hanging over the edge of the bed, I reach for George's flashlight, which stands upright under his bedtable. I hesitate to turn it on, for fear of the mouse parts that I imagine may by now be arrayed on the floor. But when I do, there is nothing there. I make my way to the one other bedroom that has a mattress, on tiptoe, the better to avoid stepping on something untoward, and lie down on the bed, shimmying futilely against the implacable mound of horsehair that presses into the small of my back. Within minutes, Mariah joins me. And then Murray! With the squealing mouse! But when he sets it down, it scampers out of the room.

Seven A.M. Light pours through the windows. Mariah nestles at my side, a round, tortoise-shell throw pillow. Murray bounds into the room and onto the bed. I duck, assuming he has brought me a piece of mouse. But no.

I tread watchfully through the morning, looking tentatively into closets, under furniture.

"Don't worry," I am told. "You'll find it when it starts to smell."

Christ, it's cold. Well, maybe not cold. But 55 degrees when you're used to 85 or 95 is hard to ignore. I pull on a long-sleeved white cotton turtleneck, then head, bare-legged, for the bureau in my alternate bedroom, where I have stored my long khaki pants. I glance out the window by the bedroom door, then shrink against the wall. Below, in the driveway, is a group of men clustered around a truck.

I retreat to the bureau, still facing the window. Somehow they won't be able to see me if I don't turn my back on them. I pull my trousers out of the drawer and yank them, somewhat clumsily, over one leg, then the other, then approach the window again. It is Mike Kravik and his men. They wear plaid flannel shirts over their T-shirts and drink coffee from oversized paper cups. I didn't know they were coming today.

"Good morning," I call out, descending the steps of my porch. No one says a word. Mike Kravik gives me a vacant look, as though he's never seen me before, as though the fact of my existence is a matter of utter indifference, even somehow unacceptable. Such a change from the other day when he came over with the samples.

"I like to do something a little different," he had said. He sifted through the samples, considering one, and then another.

"This blue is nice."

He touched the tips of his fingers to the gritty surface of the shingle material, then held it out to me, revealing, perhaps inadvertently, the gentle side in him that cares about color.

Now, three sturdy backs remain turned. I can glimpse a beard, a paunch, a cigarette dangling from a pair of lips.

"It's cold today," I say cheerily. "My furnace kicked on this morning."

Mike Kravik nods, almost imperceptibly. From the others there is no reply. I feel like a female reporter who has won a court order to be in the Mets locker room.

After breakfast, I step off the porch again. In that moment a burst of shingles soars off the roof and splats onto the walk at my feet.

"You're on your own, lady," I mutter to myself.

I dart across the driveway and watch with Mike Kravik as the men continue to pry off the shingles. They use what Kravik refers to as "Shingle-Eaters," a cross between a shovel and a spatula, whose handle pole extends into the flat of its scalloped blade.

Alone, Kravik is more approachable. Still, I sense that he is conscious of the fact that his men can see us from the roof, and doesn't know quite what to do with me.

"How much do shingles weigh?" I ask him.

"About 240 pounds per 100 square feet."

"How much weight do you suppose is on the roof now?"

"Well, I'll be putting on a single layer that will total about 4,000 pounds. And there are two layers up there now."

He turns to leave, oversee other jobs.

8,000 pounds. It is inconceivable to me that my house has been able to support 8,000 pounds. If I'd known a month ago that that's what it was doing, I probably would have slept on the lawn.

I am struck as I pull into the driveway by the boards of my roof deck, once hidden by dark layers of shingle, now giving

themselves, pristine, to the light of this September afternoon. A ladder stands on the walk at the foot of the steps of
my porch. It is rigged with a gasoline-powered hoist and a
trolley to lift the rolls of tar paper, the new shingles, to the
men on the roof. On the far side of the house, the front slope
of the roof looms black, the tar paper already installed. I
squeeze past the ladder and enter the house. Upstairs, I find
Murray and Mariah, noses to the base of the attic door, sizing
up the thud of footfalls, the resonant crack of hammer blows.

George liked to see people hell-bent in pursuit of their
interests. Whatever the odds, he certainly pursued his own.
He had one of the worst seats of anyone I ever saw on a horse.
But he managed to stay on, over fences in the hunting field,
or on the spooked and bucking cow pony in a Colorado
mountain pasture. He took a temperamentally unpromising
dachshund and turned her into the first dachshund American Kennel Club Field Trial Champion of Record. (I haven't
sought to determine whether the fact that he co-wrote the
dachshund Field Trial Rules had some bearing on his
success.) And in his tiller-steered, 1903 Prescott Steamer,
built in Passaic, New Jersey, by a firm specializing in stove
polish, he became the first American to complete the London to Brighton Veteran Car Run in his own, American, car.

The idea of the Brighton Run is irresistible. It commemorates the London to Brighton Emancipation Run of 1896, itself a celebration of the Locomotives on Highways Act of the same year, raising the speed limit to fourteen miles an hour and rescinding the requirement that a "road locomotive" in motion be preceded by a person on foot. Until 1878, the law required that the person on foot carry a red flag. Shortly before he was to sail, the Prescott caught fire. George loaded it onto the *Queen Elizabeth* as planned, and spent the days preceding the event overseeing a new paint job in a North London garage. The Run is quintessentially British. It is not a race. The aim is to get to Brighton by four o'clock, at a *maximum* average speed of twenty miles an hour (pushing by passengers allowed). George made the fifty-seven-mile run in six and a half hours.

George enjoyed danger.

"I lost my brakes going down a hill," he once told me, describing a meet on Long Island. "And at the bottom of the hill was a four-lane highway."

He paused for a moment and smiled.

"The intersection got closer and closer. I kept pumping the brakes, but with no result. I couldn't stop. All I could do was hang on."

He paused again, smiled, stared into my eyes.

"Finally, I just shot through, and when I got to the other side I was still intact!" He laughed giddily.

"And all the while I was thinking to myself, 'If only Laurie were here.' I knew you would have loved it too."

And I would have.

There were clues I didn't recognize at the time to George's impending death. Because of a recent plane crash, he decided it would be safer to take the Concorde to Paris. He had never worried about plane crashes before. We took what proved to be our last ride together in the Stanley. The car was steaming beautifully, pumps, oil and water gauges functioning well. It was one of those rides in which everything comes together. But George was fretful. What if something went wrong? He urged me to turn back. This was not the George I knew.

My reading gave me insights into my feelings after George died, even triggered understandings of what had been locked in my subconscious. I was in bed one night, propped against my pillows, Iris Murdoch's *The Book and the Brotherhood* resting against my thighs. One of the characters awoke from a dream, recalled the wise, gentle, witty eyes of a beloved lost bird, the sad, pathetic figure of his father, recently dead. "There were partings," he realized, "there were endings, there were precious things which went away forever." The words lifted me upright. Partings. Endings. Precious things which went away forever. I felt my throat tighten. It was two months since George died and I had not yet absorbed the fact that this parting, this ending, this most precious thing which had gone away, was forever.

I had been protected at first by a sense of his presence. He had died, yes, but we had been together only days before. The conscious mind knows he will not be back. But the subconscious senses that he will. In two months, his nearness had scarcely faded. Not until now did I look forever in the eye.

I copied the words onto a piece of message paper, put it on the hall table. I would stop, let the words course through me, intensify the pain that meant he was still there, inside of me. I cherished those words, and the writer whose wisdom had set them down for me. Who had made my sorrow a part of something larger than myself.

In Penelope Lively's *Moon Tiger,* the narrator, a successful popular historian, lies dying. She recalls the love of her youth, the brief interlude with the British tank commander in World War II, killed in the North African desert before their life together could begin.

"We are no longer in the same story," she says to him, in her thoughts. "You are left behind, in another place and another time, and I am someone else . . . a stranger, inhabiting a world you would not recognize."

I remember lifting my eyes from the page. Long, shallow pans of strawberry JELL-O, rice pudding, tapioca were ranged side by side in the case behind the counter at the diner. I saw myself with sparse, graying hair, having lived another life, having left George behind. I pushed the image away.

"She has gone on without him," Anne Tyler said in her review of *Moon Tiger.*

I will not go on without George. I will not lose what we have together. And perhaps I will not outlive him by so very long.

The water report arrived today. No fecal coliform. No fecal streptococci. Such a wealth of possibilities I've been unaware of. pH 7.45. Nitrate: 1.32 milligrams per liter, maximum acceptable, 10; chlorides 2.6 milligrams, maximum acceptable, 250; sulfates 2.4, maximum 250; iron .03, maximum .3. No copper, detergent, manganese, ammonia. Alkalinity 87 milligrams; total salts in solution 308; phosphates 2.03; hardness 107 (for these no standard has been set). There are no remarks in the REMARKS column. This means, according to the summary at the top of the page, that my water is "drinkable and reasonably normal." I can't help but think that since I did so well on nitrate, chlorides, sulfates, and iron I deserve more than "drinkable and reasonably normal." But no matter. I've never seen Murray drink anything. But I guess I can take Mariah off of bottled water.

The smooth slopes of charcoal gray shingle, the narrow aluminum strips of roof edging, glazed white, give my house a trimness I would have thought impossible a month ago. The coating on the flat roof of the kitchen gleams silver in the sun.

"We found a three-foot hole in the decking," Mike Kravik tells me. "But I won't charge you for the new lumber."

"That's very nice. Thank you."

The familiar twinge of alarm is muted now. Still, I wonder how a three-foot hole could have gone unnoticed for so long.

"Have you fixed it so water won't get in where the kitchen meets the house? I'm worried about my leak."

"We put in new flashing. You shouldn't have any more trouble."

"What *is* flashing exactly?"

"Well, in this case, we put a sheet of metal under the sidewall shingles along the roof line and over the roofing material on the roof. Then we covered the metal with more roofing material."

"How did you attach the roofing material?"

"Torched it on with an 18,000-BTU torch."

Kravik and his men pull away in their trucks and I revel for a moment in the clean line of my roof. Then I turn to remove the Twinkies wrappers and the Pepsi cans that have been stuffed into the groundhog holes, the crumpled cigarette packages that have been tucked into the trees.

From the train window now, in and out of New York, I look at roofs. The sloping shingled roofs of houses, the flat roofs, even recessed flat roofs, of warehouses, some covered with stones. How do they handle the drainage, I ask myself, of the flat ones, even more so of the recessed flat ones. The predominant color of the shingled roofs is gray. I look especially to see if the shingles are cut off clean just beyond the horizontal roof edge, as on my garage, or whether they droop over the horizontal edge like the ones on my new porch. The roofs of even the most humble houses are in good condition. Only recently conscious of my roof, I feel I've only recently been let in on a secret that everyone else has known all along.

After someone dies, you think of the things you have or haven't said, all the things you have or haven't done. Only the wisest among us lead our lives as though each day may be our last—or our last together. I was soon tormented after George died by remembered outbursts of impatience, of annoyance over trivialities—his repeated spilling of pipe tobacco, his neglecting to close the ice box door. A week to the day before his heart attack, we took the Metroliner to

Washington, to see the Georgia O'Keeffe show at the National Gallery, and to see my brother and his wife and their two young sons. The chintz-filled suite I had reserved at the Hay-Adams looked out over Lafayette Park to the White House. Chuck, my brother, and his older son Marc arrived at six. We would see Cathy and Tommy, the sixteen-month-old, the next day. The restaurant was only blocks away. I decided we would walk. But blocks are longer in Washington than I remembered, and it was colder than I had thought. George began to tire, and finally slipped, face-flat, on a small patch of ice. Chuck and I helped him to his feet. I watched for taxis on the street, trying to listen as Chuck and Marc chatted, trying not to make too much of George's fall. He lagged behind, as he often preferred to do. I felt his humiliation. Why hadn't I had the sense, or was it the thoughtfulness, to get a cab?

For weeks, months, after he died, I was haunted by the image of him sprawled on the sidewalk, gray tweed overcoat fanning outward, elbows bent, closed hands pushing against the cement. Had I been right in those last years to treat his aging as I did? Had I taken good enough care of him? He didn't like to be fussed over. I could sometimes take his hand, and we would walk, as lovers do, my arm ready to stiffen with any loss of balance. But, as often, he would shake loose of me, make his way on his own. And I felt that to fuss too much was to point up a frailty that neither of us wanted to acknowledge. To treat him as though he were younger would make him so.

In my moments of guilt and doubt I would turn to the contentment of our last week together. Traveling back the next day on the train, after following two young boys through the Air and Space Museum, the new museum of African art, I brought coffee and two giant chocolate chip cookies from the café car. The expression on George's face told me he approved of my choice. I remember him removing the plastic wrap, sipping his coffee, breaking off chunks of cookie. We were together, the two of us, the effort of the day behind us. He was so handsome there beside me.

The following Tuesday we heard Verdi's *Macbeth* at the Met. Although not an opera enthusiast, he had come often, to please me. The performance was a surprise to him, how much he enjoyed it, became absorbed in it. The next day, he hired a car to take him to New Jersey, to visit an antique car collection, and came home full of its excellence, his excitement. He bubbled again on the phone to a friend about the ambulance drivers lowering him delirious out the window of our hotel room in Paris, like a piano. They'd done no such thing, of course, but it made the story better.

I would remind myself of the night at the theater the previous July, James Earl Jones in *Fences*, George's younger son Jack, with his wife and two children, visiting from California. We had gotten tickets at the last minute and so were scattered through the balcony, George and Jack on the aisle, the rest of us toward the center of our respective rows. As the curtain came down, George leapt out of his seat, making his way out of the auditorium and down the stairs to the lobby. Jack trailed after him, reaching out to make sure he didn't fall, but George would have none of it. As he pushed his way through the lobby doors and onto the street, I caught up with them, Jack stepped aside. I put one hand on George's shoulder. He turned. His face opened. "There you are," he exclaimed, his eyes bright with relief, and joy.

But there was no ultimate reassurance. I was tortured by the fact that I hadn't had a chance to say goodbye. To put into words what a difference he had made in my life, how proud I was of him, how I treasured him. By the time I knew he would die, it was too late.

"We have to go now," I said to him, long after visiting hours were over, on the evening of his heart attack.

"I'll go with you," he said.

"I'm afraid you can't tonight. You're stuck."

I brushed a strand of hair off of his forehead.

"I'm not stuck," he said. "You're stuck."

"No, I'm not."

"Yes, you are," he insisted. "You're stuck with me."

The words poured out urgently. "I love being stuck with you," I said. "I can't think of anything I want more."

He closed his eyes. Said nothing more.

I ask myself now, Was that enough? Did he hear what I was saying? It had been the spontaneous response of one caught off guard, answering from the heart before the brain had gathered the self-possession to frame better words. And I had wanted to say more. But I was self-conscious in the presence of the others. There would be other chances.

At the time, I knew he understood. But later, when it became so important, when he had died, I ached with wanting to be sure. We had often made ourselves understood to one another through the camouflage of humor, of ironic understatement. But did he understand this time? Did he understand that "I love being stuck with you" meant simply "I love you, and I want to take care of you"? He was gone now. And I hadn't uttered the precise, explicit, simple words.

On George's second day at the hospital, Jack and I sat for a while in the waiting room, in large, metal-armed leather chairs.

"You know," he said to me, "Fa told me last summer, 'I hope you've gotten as much out of your marriage as I've gotten out of mine. After all these years, I finally know what love and happiness is.' "

I hug the words to me, hope that he actually said them, hope that they are true.

Wayne and Paul have left off installing new casing around my Dutch door, and the three of us peer into the back of Glenn's Chevy Hi-Cube Van. In the dark interior of the truck, an eleven-and-three-quarter-inch sheet of aluminum unrolls from a coil and feeds into the far end of an oblong box, then slowly extrudes from the end facing us in the form of a gutter, which balances on a tripod standing ten or fifteen feet behind the truck.

"What's inside the box?" Wayne asks Glenn. "Some sort of rollers?"

"That's right," Glenn replies. As the gutter lengthens, he adds a second tripod, ten or fifteen feet beyond the first.

"How much do you get out of one of those coils?"

"About fifteen hundred feet." Glenn grins. "I'm always afraid that if I leave the machine on while I go into the house or something, I'll get distracted and come out to find seamless gutter extending a quarter of a mile down the road."

When the gutter has reached thirty-six feet, he turns off the machine and the gutter comes to rest. He saws it off with a hacksaw, then with a hole punch cuts a hole to accommodate the drain, and with a crimper secures the prefabricated aluminum ends. He places "hidden hangers," a sort of square bracket lying on its back, two feet apart against the inside top edges, inserts a screw through each bracket foot and partway through the back of the gutter, then lifts the gutter at its center and carries it, a majestic almost eighteen-foot droop to either side, up a ladder where, driving home the screws with a battery-powered drill, he fastens it to the fascia board along the side of my porch. As a one-man show it is almost without equal.

A contractor pulls in, climbs out of his truck. He is working on a house down the road.

"Are you coming tomorrow?" he asks Glenn. "It's going

to rain tomorrow night and I promised this guy he'd have gutters before it rains."

A burly man, he inhales, and his chest swells, as he readies himself to protest the answer he fears he is about to receive.

"I'll be there," Glenn assures him. The contractor relaxes, exhales.

Glenn jumps to the ground and pulls his ladder away from the porch.

"I've got a job in Summit tomorrow too," he says, "but I'll just have to blow him off."

I avert my face, to suggest I haven't been listening, assuming this is an expression a woman isn't meant to hear.

Once Glenn has finished, with gutters along the front and the side of my porch, along the back of the kitchen, new downspouts in place, old downspouts extended, the gutters excite me as I have not been excited by the new porch or the new roof. I try to contain my enthusiasm in front of Wayne. The graceful line of the gutters, the creamy glow of their enamel, create an air of something fine. So adorned, my house resembles the faded lady whose new pearl choker makes her feel beautiful enough to go to the ball.

I woke up again this morning terrified. That's nothing new. But it was worse this time. I got up, had breakfast, drove the Suburban to New York. It wasn't until I arrived that I stopped shaking. Or was confident I wouldn't start to scream. What is it that is making me so afraid?

One reads about the stages of grief. Disbelief. Guilt. Anger. Resignation. Acceptance. The progression, of course, is not so neat. I never consciously disbelieved that George had died. Unless it could be said that until I confronted the concept of "forever" I didn't truly believe that he was dead. The guilt came only days after he had died. And comes on me still. As does the anger.

Driving my Rabbit from New York to New Jersey, in the weeks and months after George died, I would leave the garage at 87th and Lexington, cross the park at 85th, travel down West End Avenue to the Lincoln Tunnel. The anger, the sense of injustice, the sense of having been betrayed, the waste would well up in my chest and my throat until, speeding away from the toll booth onto the turnpike, I would burst into tears, raging at what I saw as George's destruction of the unprecedented bond that we had shared. This was not the anger I had so often heard spoken of, the anger of the spouse who feels abandoned. A husband, reading in an armchair, slumps over, dies. His wife rushes to his chair, grabs his lapels, shakes him with all her strength. "Don't you dare leave me," she screams. But one cannot be angry at someone for dying. Very few of us choose to die.

My anger was anger at a betrayal of the deepest trust, at an earlier, different form of abandonment, the period, beginning about a year after we were married, during which George fell in love with himself.

It was his defense, really, against the humiliation of no longer having enough money to lead the life he had led. (I was paying a significant portion of his expenses myself.) It was the result of a devotion to the idea of family that ended, too often, in smugness and self-delusion. And it was the result of an understanding of marriage as competition. For nearly a year, I was no longer "the most wonderful thing that had happened in his life," but the undeserving intruder who had presumed to marry a Schieffelin.

The ways in which his feelings manifested themselves seem so trivial in the retelling. The look of contempt when I expressed a desire to use my grandmother's heavy Victorian flat silver, rather than the reproduction colonial pattern of the 1920s that had been chosen by his first wife, and which he deemed in better taste. His response when I suggested the possibility that a cousin of mine had been with him in "the first class at Quonset," a group of prominent investment bankers, business and professional men, recruited under the aegis of Under Secretary of the Navy James Forrestal, to bring additional management talent into the navy at the start of World War II: "Oh, that's impossible," he said. "That was a very select group of people." The withering comments in the company of his children. At a family gathering, he proposed that the big house be sold without the 200 acres it sat on. "I wouldn't think anyone would want to buy a house of this size without the land," I said. "What do you know," he replied. "No one in your family ever had 200 acres." His mock cringe when his son Jack observed unwittingly (to me, the mostly Scottish Annie Laurie Graham), "The Scotch were nothing but a bunch of troublemakers." "The Quakers were troublemakers too," I retorted. George's cringe turned to fury. "What counts is the money," he spluttered, shaking with disdain. Hannah Lawrence's family had had plenty of money.

He would strut around the apartment, chest puffed out like a bantam cock's, glorying in his bloodlines. Only when I took him on a tour of my own family did he shut up. My cousin had indeed been in the same class at Quonset. My aunt and uncle had five times as much land as he had. The more he learned, the more he boasted about me. But it was too late. I like to think that now I would brush off such puerile assaults. But I hadn't been good enough either for the one other central person in my life—my mother. And I had loved him so defenselessly. His look of disgust was more than I could bear. I never completely forgave him. It closed off a part of me. It made me less patient. And although I loved him, it was more warily.

I understand it all now, better than I understood it then. The intense, parochial snobbery of the world he grew up in. And his own fear of rejection. His parents hadn't had as much money as many of their friends. His flunking out of

Princeton had been an intellectual and social humiliation scarcely spoken of above a whisper. His father had been a continuing embarrassment, his mother a paragon impossible to live up to. He worried, baselessly, even a few years ago, that he might be dropped from his automobile clubs. Behind the wit, the kindness, the worldliness, lurked the dread of not measuring up. Without enough money, he fell back on ancestry, as a mark of superiority and not as a call to responsibility for those less blessed. It was ancestry as a justification of unkindness. I had not encountered it before. And it left me desperate. Because of the anguish of rejection, of being thought unworthy, somehow unclean. And because his capacity for petty cruelty threatened to diminish him so much in my eyes.

"I finally know what love and happiness is," he said to Jack. By that time, of course, it was I who had the upper hand. But I didn't take advantage of it. It was perhaps only then that he realized that marriage is not a competition, that he truly understood what it was to be safe in the arms of someone you love.

Ha! The rain is teeming. A perfect time to check my new gutters. I pull up the hood of my rain suit and head down the stairs of my porch. To my right, water pours from the downspout that parallels the sloping metal doors of my cellar. At the front of the house, another downspout peeks from under the wisteria. Water flows here too. I flush with pleasure at the principles of the science of mechanics made manifest in my yard.

Then I hear it, the slap of water against earth. I round the far corner of the house. Toward the rear, water cascades over the roof edge, in a jagged fringe that coalesces into sharp-pointed pencil columns that could be coursing from a spigot. For some reason the rainwater isn't flowing into the gutter drain. Only a trickle comes out of the downspout. And the falling water is carving a crevasse in the newly seeded bank of topsoil that Ed has just built up along the side of the house.

It is Saturday afternoon. The wind blows pellets of rain against my face. I'll never get Mike Kravik now.

At the hardware store I find a large, electric blue, polyethylene tarp. Ed has bought me some of those flipper-shaped things that you put under downspouts to protect the grass. I'd like to get more, to place under the spigot-falls of water. But they have only one—not like what Ed has brought, but an overblown object, made of plastic that has been fashioned to suggest the surface of a rock, but which makes me think of the gular pouch of an iguana.

"It's so ugly," I protest, uselessly.

"Do you want it?" the sales clerk asks.

"I suppose so."

He removes it from the wall display and hands it to me.

"It's so light."

"You're supposed to fill it with water or sand."

The label calls it a Lawn Saver.

The tarp crackles as I shake it out and, fighting the wind, lay it like a bedsheet over the topsoil. I secure it with a slab of slate that, until Ed filled it in, had sat over the circular hole containing the plumbing controls to the fountain, and with a cinderblock that, to no apparent purpose, lay by the crawl space under the laundry room. My foot sinks into gumbo and I lurch sideways, steadying myself against the side of the house. A jet of falling water catches the hood of my jacket and rips it off my head. Water pours down the back of my neck.

I fill the Lawn Saver from the hose in the garage and lug it clumsily to the side of the house. I had no idea it would be so heavy. As I start up the bank, my foot slips and I stumble forward, the Lawn Saver thudding to the ground beneath me. Thrashing about with my tarps, staggering and sliding through the mud, I imagine my neighbors sniggering behind their curtains at the loon who lives next door. But I just got all this topsoil! I can't let it wash away!

One lone red leaf amidst the green clarions the approach of autumn from the maple by my garage. It occurs to me that if I let the mason know how small my job really is, he'll be more inclined to fit me in—before it snows. The foundation is accessible on only one side of the house, as the wall that forms the railing of my porch runs along the front and the other side, and the back is abutted by the box that is my kitchen. When I tell him that the outside measurement is only thirty-two feet, he seems surprised—and more accommodating.

From there on, the news goes downhill.

"The framing under your kitchen door is full of termites," Wayne tells me. I have pushed the thought of an exterminator to the back of my mind, even in the face of the ants, who, in spite of Ed's spraying, appear to be immortal. I have enough workmen to think about already, and maybe what I don't know won't hurt me. But now the evidence is at hand.

The lady of the house on the lot behind my garage approaches while I am outside with Mike Kravik.

"You've met the rest of the family," she says with a smile. "I just wanted to introduce myself. I'm Gloria Danforth."

She wears a blue velours sweatshirt and matching pants.

"It's our house's turn to be hit by lightning this year," she remarks.

This interests me.

"But you're the one who's really had trouble."

"Oh?"

"Your house has been hit at least once, and there used to be a tree right there." She points to the other side of the driveway. "It got hit four times and finally had to be chopped down."

That explains one of my holes.

"And there was a schoolhouse across the road that burned to the ground. You're in a great place."

This is clearly a chapter in my house's history it's been just as well I didn't know.

Now what! Peacefully eating my breakfast, minding my own business. I pick up the morning's *Times*. On the front page, I find that I live eleven miles from what, until they cleaned it up, was considered "the worst [known] residential radon hotspot" in the nation. I rummage through the pile of papers on the desk in the sewing room for the *Times* article of a year ago that I had cut out and saved. Here it is. "All residents of Sussex, Warren and Hunterdon Counties and portions of eight other counties are being urged by the State Environmental Protection Commissioner to have their homes tested for radon 'as soon as practical.' " As soon as practical. I had saved the article. It was hard not to be somewhat concerned. But it had not been hard, in the end, to ignore it. Every time you turn around you're eating or inhaling some new carcinogen. But I live here full-time now. And my father died of lung cancer. Worst residential radon hotspot. At the end of the article is a toll-free number. I start dialing.

A large manila envelope arrives from the State of New Jersey, Department of Environmental Protection, Division of Environmental Quality, Bureau of Environmental Radiation. Inside are a letter, two booklets, two pages of radon testing information, and a list of testing firms. On the sheet of testing information I am struck above all by the paragraph on water. "If the radon in air measurement is above 4.0 pCi/ l *and* you have a private well, you may wish to test your water for radon. . . . Radon is released from water when it is agitated or heated, as in showers. . . . To date, no guidelines have been recommended for the concentration of radon in water."

I start taking shorter showers, breathing more shallowly, turning my back on the water as often as possible. I can see radon in the steam. Lewis tells me I can get a radon test kit at the hardware store. I must do it today.

Two husky young men in T-shirts and blue jeans shovel the bank of topsoil from the far side of my house. They are here to point up my foundation. In the driveway, Stan and his brother Gary take on water in the big tanks of their truck, fill the portable duster, prepare their drills. They are here to rid my house of carpenter ants and termites.

"I hope the masons won't be in your way," I say to Stan. "I had no idea they were coming today."

"No problem," he replies. "We'll work around each other."

In their crisp navy trousers and shirts, Stan and Gary are the nattiest of the people who have worked on my house. They are an engaging pair. Stan, the shorter of the two, is solid, with thick auburn hair and trim beard, a merry person with a quick, hearty laugh. Gary is taller, slender, a bit more reserved. His mouth curves slightly as he starts to speak. They enjoy their profession, and they play off one another, alternating sentences in reply to my questions.

"How can you tell if wood has been infested by carpenter ants or by termites?" I ask. It wasn't until Stan and Gary came to give me an estimate and detected signs of carpenter ant infestation that it occurred to me those were carpenter ants in the wisteria. (I had forgotten completely about the carpenter ants in the porch posts.)

"Carpenter ants are looking for a home," Stan replies. "They hollow out galleries, leave a trail of sawdust."

"A termite wouldn't dream of leaving sawdust," Gary continues. "That's his food."

"A termite is also bringing in soil," Stan adds, "to replace the wood he's taken out. He has to keep everything damp or he'll die."

"So that's a sign of termite infestation? Soil in the wood?"

"Right. The methods we use are different too," Stan explains. "We're actually killing the carpenter ants, with insecticide. With termites we're creating a chemical barrier that prevents them from getting into the house."

"Why don't you kill the termites too?"

"There will always be termites in the soil. You can't kill them all. That's why we establish a barrier."

"Does that mean there are termites left in the house after the treatment?"

"Yes, it does. But it also means they can no longer go back and forth."

"Once the wood dries out," Gary interjects, "they die."

Gary sets to work on the carpenter ants, drilling through the siding with a quarter-inch drill bit, pumping Diaznon 2D, a chemical dust, into the holes, then plugging them with tapered wooden dowels. Inside the house, Mariah and Murray sniff at the hammer blows, the bite of the drill, along the wall, from one room to another, then upstairs. In my bedroom, Murray sits on the needlepoint footstool, cranes his neck around the sheer white curtain, to get a closer look at Gary, standing now on the porch roof, boring holes into the outside walls, pumping, hammering in the plugs. I recall Murray's mouse, which I have never found.

Stan trenches the soil and drills half-inch holes in the concrete at the rear of the house, in the floor of my porch. Uncoiling the hose from the motor-driven pump on their truck, he injects Dragnet FT, a mixture of Permethrin and water, to establish the chemical barrier against termites. Then he refills the holes with concrete, replaces the soil. Inside the house, with a portable stainless tank, he sprays Dursban 2E along the baseboards, and in the cellar, to pick up any carpenter ants who might stray into the house. It could take three weeks for all of them to die. He has promised that the chemicals won't hurt the cats, but the odor and the ominous liquid along the periphery of my floors are not reassuring.

When they have finished, they present me with a Termite Guarantee Certificate, stating that for five years my "dwelling" will remain free of termites. The certificate is pale green, with a darker green engraved border, and it is signed and dated. My name has been typed at the top. This impressive document seems gleefully incongruous in the context of my house. But, in fact, hard as it is to believe, once the insulation is done, my house should be, if far from beautiful, at least certifiably safe and sound. Maybe it won't even fall down.

A rush of heat curls my gut, and I just manage to stifle the whimper that rises in my throat. The large blue block letters at the top of the sheet read NOTICE. I have taken it from the pile of identical notices that lies on the counter at the newsstand. I feel the eyes of the other customers on me, as if they can see through my clothes. "It is extremely important," the text reads, "that the residents along the county road be aware that the perspective of certain township and county officials is that the road should eventually be *widened to four (4) lanes.*" My heart crashes in my chest. All I have left of George is my house. And now they are going to take it away.

I stand in my kitchen, arms resting on the lower section of the Dutch door, looking out across the grass, unruffled beneath a benign September sun. Would it be possible for me to stay? What about all the construction? Would the new road come right up to my porch? In my mind's eye I see big yellow bulldozers clawing up my earth, leveling everything in their path.

Where would I go? It would cost a fortune to buy a decent house. And to build a garage. I don't even want to. I need time to decide what I'm going to do with my life.

Someday Paris will be another home. But not yet. We hadn't even moved into the apartment there. It is here that George is with me—in his chair, at his desk, in the bed that we shared. He is the garage, and the cars, the walls of this house. When I walk along the driveway, he walks with me.

When I watch the train pull into the station, he watches with me. I am wrapped in his presence. He is still my life. I cannot leave. I am not ready to move on.

George wouldn't have chosen Paris. He had lived in France, but too long ago. He could no longer summon the bravado to deal with another, more sophisticated, culture, and one reaches an age at which one simply prefers to stay home. But he went along with it for me.

My France was the product as much of my imagination as of experience. It was the France of language and of literature—the pellucid *alexandrins* of Racine, the *mot juste* of Flaubert. I empathized, even identified, with her misfits—Chateaubriand's René at the mouth of Etna, Proust and his goodnight kiss and his cork-lined walls. (Well, maybe not the cork-lined walls.) Snug in South Hadley, Massachusetts, I delighted in the gloom of Baudelairean spleen. *"Pluviôse, irrité contre la ville entière."* I loved the extended low growl of the word *"Pluviôse."* I loved the language. And I could only feel drawn to a country in which language, and the life of the mind, are so prized.

But I had spent comparatively little time there. And it wasn't until after a years-long attack of anglophilia that I decided George and I should go to Paris. It didn't take long. By the time we reached the hotel, I knew we had come to the center of the universe. I felt my life take a turn. Someday I would have an apartment here. Before long, the family sold Scribners. I was free again to spend my money as I wished. I had quit my job. We could travel back and forth. Paris would be my next dream.

"Am I being foolish?" I asked George, over chicken salad at the bistro on Madison Avenue. "I know hardly anyone there. And I don't even know the city that well. It's a big investment. The government might not let me take the money back out."

"You're not being foolish," he said. "And don't worry what might happen if."

In the October before the January he died, we went apartment-hunting, staying in the studio of a friend, on the Avenue Montaigne, a broad, tree-lined avenue, whose opulent buildings house the salons of some of the world's great couturiers—Jean-Louis Scherrer, Nina Ricci, Christian Dior. But this was not the Paris I wanted to live in, and each morning, after picking up fresh croissants and the newspapers for George, I would head by taxi down the Avenue Montaigne, to the Place de l'Alma, the Eiffel Tower rising beyond, then left along the Seine to the Place de la Concorde, across the Pont de la Concorde, past the Palais Bourbon, and down the Boulevard St-Germain to the heart of the sixth arrondissement, among whose old buildings, huddled along narrow side streets, its small shops and cafés, I hoped to find a home.

I could afford thirty-five to fifty square meters (thirty-five square meters being about the size of the studio I rented when I first came to New York). And I soon learned the variety of configurations that range of square meters could take. I saw looming rectangular spaces, isosceles triangles, parallelograms, new moons. A studio on the Seine had five tall windows facing Notre-Dame, but they were about to install a kitchen in the center of the opposite wall, where a fireplace should have been, and you had to cross an unheated landing to get to the narrow, gently curving!, bathroom. A sixth-floor *grenier* near the Seine, with elevator, overlooked the rooftops of the city in a view that rivaled a postcard, but the apartment was shaped like a boomerang, and the outer walls sloped inward, leaving a minimum of headroom.

Many apartments looked out onto quiet courtyards that hid behind the imposing closed doors of the buildings' façades. Most of the apartments had been renovated. The larger ones in my price range needed to be. Renovated bathrooms and kitchens tended to be gaudy. And except for those windows looking out on Notre-Dame, there was little in the way of architectural detail.

What I took to be a miracle appeared, not in the sixth, but on the Ile St-Louis, in a seventeenth-century building, a studio with a sensible layout, fireplace, walls lined with bookshelves, dark massive beams. I saw it at 1:30, called the agent with an offer at 4:00, only to learn that a young man had seen it just after I had, and had already made an offer. I had been told that one had to move fast in Paris. Now I knew.

But there was another miracle. In the rue St-Sulpice,

near St-Sulpice Church. Only blocks from the Odéon
theater, from the Luxembourg Gardens, from number 12,
rue de l'Odéon, former site of Sylvia Beach's Shakespeare
and Company. The streets were dotted with publishers, with
rare book and print dealers. Oysters and crabs, other *fruits de
mer*, were displayed in stalls outside cheerful, unpretentious
restaurants. And behind the simple façade of a seventeenth-
century house, a winding staircase led to the *troisième étage*,
and the forty square meters of my apartment-to-be.

The door was open and I could see immediately the
graceful carved stone fireplace. The tall, and somewhat
crooked, casement windows looked out on a row of houses
that could have been a stage set for *La Bohème*. The apartment had a living room, with alcove, and a bedroom. The
rooms were small, but the walls were white. The diminutive
kitchen and the bathroom had been renovated in muted
earth tones, and white. There was even a window in the
kitchen. And light. A perfect blend of the old and the new.
I made an offer on the spot.

George's eyes were bright with my excitement, as I
babbled about what I had found. I called the bank in New
York, to ask them to wire the funds I needed to the account
I had opened in Paris. As I recited account and telex
numbers, George interrupted. They should take half the
money from his account. We would buy the apartment
together.

The next day I took him to see it. He hardly bothered to
hide his dismay. Granted, the stucco on the exterior of the

building was badly in need of repair and there was a bulge in one corner of the façade. The interior was anything but spacious. But George liked things that impressed. He didn't understand the allure of bohemia, however expensive bohemia might be in the sixth!

On our next trip, in December, and before George landed in the Paris hospital, we waited, as one waits in New York, for the telephone company to install the phone. We sat on the gray-carpeted floor, read the Paris *Herald, Maison et Jardin,* looked out the windows, paced back and forth. Finally, the installer arrived. Minutes later, our unfurnished apartment was no longer unfurnished. We had a phone. It sat there, on the floor in the living room, beige with over-sized sans serif numerals, the height of French style. We stood over it, in silence. This was our phone. It legitimized us in some way. It linked us to this place. I could feel George's sudden rush of affection for what had just become our home away from home.

When I am ready, I will go back. And I will be filled with gratitude that he had shared its beginnings with me. However impractical, he had wanted me to buy it, had helped me to buy it. He had wanted me to chase this dream.

Well, back to square one. Rain thrashes my house. Thunder crashes. And water pours from the lintel between the dining room and the kitchen. I put a bucket under the worst of the flow, and mop the floor with a handful of rags. So much for flashing.

But I am not so naïve anymore. I am almost sure that the back window of the bedroom over the dining room sits directly above the doorway into the kitchen. Once the rain has stopped, I go outside to look.

"You were right, Laurie," Wayne says. "We found an opening between the drip cap and the sidewall shingles. But we've caulked it. You shouldn't have any more trouble."

I may yet become the mistress of this house.

Nothing's ever easy. I got my radon test kit, not from the hardware store, nor from the county Extension Center, to which I was sent by the hardware store, but at the Health Department, where the women behind the counter flatly informed me they had no kits, until a man appeared on the stairway over my shoulder and gave me two.

I open the aluminum-lined outer envelope and pull out the four-by-six-inch test kit packet, a wedge-shaped piece of cardboard, and a set of instructions that folds out longitudinally. I lay the instructions, unfolded, on the table by my side. They tell me to squeeze the test kit packet so that one end opens in the shape of a fish mouth, then fold the cardboard into the shape of a paper airplane and insert it, wingspan against the white inner pouch, which should be pressing against the roof of the fish mouth. When I have done so, my fish mouth refuses to stay open as wide as the one in the accompanying illustration, so I take the cardboard out and try again, but with the same result. I have some misgivings about the reliability of my test kit, but I tie a string in the hole provided at the rear exterior of the fish mouth, and suspend the packet four feet off the floor of my cellar, from one of the overhead beams, where I have found a convenient, if somewhat rusty, nail. It won't be long now.

One of the clerks in the deli tells me the "improvements" to the county road won't take place in our lifetime.

My heart sinks when I see the men from the insulation company. They, too, are country men. The one in charge wears a T-shirt that reads: "Warm your ass with fiberglass."

"We'll have to pull one of the windows and the frame out of the attic," he says, "to dispose of the old insulation."

"All right," I reply, though I can't help but wonder if they aren't simply going to wreck my house.

I sit, pretending I feel no apprehension, in an armchair

in the "sewing room," with the recently published *Letters of T. S. Eliot*. It is difficult to concentrate on the effusions of Jean Verdenal, a medical student and fellow lodger with Eliot in Paris, to whom "The Love Song of J. Alfred Prufrock" is dedicated. From outside the window, I hear a thud. I look over my shoulder. Perched on the grass of my new bank of topsoil, a ball of wadded insulation looms, four or five feet in diameter, fiberglass pink against the green. A juxtaposition worthy of an Eliot, or a Magritte. How did they fit it through the window?! Four more balls follow.

One of the men passes through the dining room and out to their truck. The other, who has remained in the attic, tosses a rope out the window to his partner, hauls up a two-and-a-half-inch, wire-reinforced rubber hose, and a control switch on its separate line. As the pre-ground fiberglass is loaded into the hopper in the truck, where it is further broken up, he operates the control switch, which releases the wiry pink tufts into the hose, and through the hose to my attic and under the floorboards. In the cellar, they remove the old insulation through the outside metal doors, and install the new, in strips, between the floor joists.

When they have finished, they load the balls of insulation into the truck, and sweep meticulously, upstairs, in the dining room, anywhere dirt may have been tracked in, or a tuft of pink may have strayed. "Warm your ass with fiberglass," so unexpectedly careful with his broom. They leave without a trace.

But the roof! Even from the foot of the attic stairs I can see the underside of the roof deck, now stripped of insulation, smeared with the black scorch of fire.

I start up the shallow, narrow steps, hands at shoulder level, palms flat against the walls of the stairwell to either side. The pale pink of the stairwell walls is gray with dirt, scuffed with brown, Crayola-like marks. I step onto the attic floor and run a finger along one of the rafters. It has the empty, brittle feel of charcoal, its glistening black surface scored with clefts and rivulets. Fingers flat against one side, thumb against the other, my hand forms a U around the board. It creaks as I squeeze. Black dust crumbles into my palm.

The entire roof deck is charred to some degree, except for the front slope on the far side of the house, where the boards have been replaced, and toward the back of the house, where Mike Kravik's boards are ghostly pale against the sooty black that surrounds them.

How could George have allowed something so unsafe? Didn't he care? Did he know? Why did he replace the boards in only one section? Maybe the worst never happens, but isn't this pushing your luck? I am angry. How could he be so cavalier? I had four men walking on that roof! What if it had caved in?

"Would it be possible for you to come and look at the damage that was done by the fire?"

Bob Beck hears the alarm in my voice.

"I'll be right over."

His smile fills my attic as he reaches the top of the stairs.

"You had a fire all right," he says.

He steps over boxes, suitcases, all dusted with black, and taps a knuckle here and there against the roof deck, grasps a rafter.

"Is it dangerous?" I ask.

"Not really," he says. "Look."

He takes a quarter out of his pocket and scrapes one of the rafters with its edge.

"See?"

Where he has scraped, I can see fresh, undamaged wood.

"But what about these?"

I point to two rafters, their squared-off edges as if melted into a series of ripples, the flat of the board sliced deep with cracks.

"And that board up there!"

At the apex of the roof, the rafters meet the charred remains of another board running half the roof's length.

"You mean the ridge? You don't have to worry about that. You don't even really need that board."

"It doesn't hold up the roof?"

"No. It's the rafters that do that, in triangulation with the ceiling beams."

"So what you think holds up a house doesn't really hold it up at all."

I look up at the ridge, mentally absorbing its diminished status.

"Do you think I need to do anything?"

"Tell you what. For your own peace of mind, ask Wayne to run new rafters alongside these particularly bad ones. And to install a few collar ties from rafter to rafter. This is where the worst of the damage took place."

"Put in . . . ?"

"Collar ties. Two-by-fours to run horizontally, from one slope to the other, at about head height. Just for reinforcement."

"Collar ties," I repeat to myself, trying to engrave the term in my mind.

With Bob gone, I marvel at the margin of safety built into a house. Those boards were supporting 8,000 pounds of shingles, and four men. The mere thought is alarming. But everything is intact. My house didn't fall down.

Two picocuries! Two only! I've passed the radon test. I'm allowed to have up to four. I think back fleetingly to the fact that my fish mouth wasn't as wide as the one in the picture. Well, someday I'll run another test. But, for now, I'll accept these results—gladly!

I woke up this morning in the cold light of dawn, immobile with the terror that is always there, waiting. I lay on my side, my back to the window, clutching a corner of pillow against my cheek. I heard the occasional rush of a car along the road below.

As the minutes went by, the terror began to churn, its elements shifting, separating, reforming, a palette of grays that I think I can recall literally being able to see—a sort of monochromatic, somehow visible, emotional kaleidoscope. The terror churned, shifted. I felt its soundless rumble. Then it came to rest, in a new configuration now, no longer terror, but simply the ache of missing George. This, then, is the true identity of my fear.

Night has fallen now when I return from the diner. I pull into the driveway, and each night I catch them, in the distance, frozen, four or five deer, poised to run, my headlights reflected in their wide frightened eyes.

George always knew what to do. I awoke one Saturday morning, early in the fall, while we were still in the big house, to a noise that sounded like the bleating of a sheep. I lay in bed listening, knowing we had no sheep, wondering what it could be. When the noise stopped, I rolled over to go back to sleep. Then it began again.

I got out of bed, put on my yellow terry cloth robe, went barefoot down the stairs and out the front door. The sun was shining, but the air was cool and there was a breeze. I looked up the gentle slope of lawn to my right, past the lilac bush, to the peeling red barn that we used as a garage, then to the left, my eyes following the outer arc of driveway that ran along the edge of the woods, curving around the apple tree, the maple, the multifurcated trunk of the magnolia, to come full circle in front of me. I saw nothing out of the ordinary, but still, at unpredictable intervals, there was that odd, somehow desperate sound.

I pushed through an opening in the hedge to my left, toward the deep end of the pool, my view of the shallow end blocked for a moment by the bulbous evergreens that bordered the terrace along the side of the house. And then I saw her, facing me across the shimmering length of blue water, a doe, half-submerged in the shallow end, wedged between the ladder and the concrete wall. She listed slightly to one side, right foreleg hooked over the top rung of the ladder, hind legs through the lower rungs, stretched toward me, rigid with her terror.

"George! There's a deer in the pool," I cried, running back up the stairs. "There's a deer in the pool."

George sat up in bed, shaking his head against the fog of sleep.

"I'll be right there," he said, heading for the bathroom.

I ran back downstairs, out the porch door this time, to the pool. Afraid of frightening her, I knelt on one knee, slightly behind her, ten or so feet to the side. She was quiet now, chin lifted, her dun-colored profile etched against the trees.

"Don't worry," I said beseechingly. "We'll get you out. Don't be afraid."

She watched me from the corner of her big, dark eye.

Alone, I too was afraid, not just of frightening her, but of going closer to that beautiful, alien creature. She inspired the fear and awe I had felt once as a child, in the presence of a man who was blind, his tragedy too huge and too incomprehensible to confront. I shrank from the surging power, the unplumbable unknown, behind those unseeing eyes.

George approached from behind, looked down at me in passing, as if to say, "What the hell are you doing?" He strode over to the deer. I followed, knelt behind her. Her back was to the wall of the pool, her left buttock on one of the lower rungs of the ladder, her hind legs extended under the surface of the water. How big she was, her trunk at least as large as mine. George reached down, touched his fingers to her brow, ran his hand over the top of her head, the back of her neck. The tension flowed out of her. With this one caress, her hind legs relaxed, sank deeper into the water, her body limp with relief, and trust.

George tore off his robe and jumped in, stood facing her in the chest-deep, frigid water. From behind, I put my hands on her sides, under her forelegs, and righted her as one would a baby, so that she sat square on the rung of the ladder. She understood what I was attempting to do, cooperated, settled herself on both buttocks. George moved to her side, took hold of her midsection, started to pull. Her hide, taut with the stored fat of a summer's browsing, scraped against the side of the pool. George pulled, in short bursts, his face tight, turning her back slightly toward him as he managed to move her, a fraction of an inch, another. He worked with a gentle but firm authority she did not question.

One hind leg pressed now against the side of the ladder. George circled around, placed one hand behind her hock, the other over the cloven hoof, pushed the leg back through the rungs of the ladder, then took hold of the other leg, pushed it back, through, leaving her wedged sideways between the ladder and the wall. Behind her now, he began to pull again, starting and stopping, the doe still unprotesting, her thigh scraping, until he wrested her from the viselike grip of concrete and metal.

"While I turn her, you lift her front legs onto the edge," George said, his voice straining as he fell backward momentarily with her weight. He held her by her chest, pushed upward, as I placed my hands behind her knees, the long slender metacarpals cradled against my wrists. I heard the damp clack of hooves against the concrete.

"Now hold onto her flanks while I push her out."

Forelegs on the ground, flanks in the air, she scrambled for footing, her hind legs collapsing momentarily as they touched the concrete. Then she stood, tentative, stiff from the cold and the confinement of the pool, took a few wobbly steps, stopped. Her haunches quivered. I sat on my heels, watching. Water glistened against her coat, the white edges of her tail. She turned, looked over her shoulder at me, in acknowledgment, her large dark eyes fixing mine. She stood, I knelt, in silence, held for a long breathless moment in a gaze, two living creatures who had faced trouble together and had won.

George climbed out of the pool, shivering, his teeth chattering, grabbed his robe.

"I'm going to have a hot shower," he said.

The doe took a few more tentative steps, then lay down, her back to me, along the row of cedars that paralleled the edge of the pool. Worried that with the breeze and her wet coat she would be cold, I took off my robe, moved toward her, on my knees.

"I just want to put this over you," I said quietly. "I don't want you to get cold."

The robe fanned over her, frightened her, and she clambered to her feet, hobbled around the line of cedars into a ruffled patch of sunlight. She lay down, her back to me again, head up, pointed ears alert. Beyond, the wine red leaves of a dogwood, the slender weeping branches of a willow lifted in the breeze. The line of her head and her neck curved gently into the length of her body, giving her the aura of a queen. I approached her again, pulling my cotton nightgown from under my knees, calling softly, my robe trailing at my side. Again I reached her, and again I covered her with the robe. This time she didn't run, but lay there, head high, shielded against the chill.

I backed away, still on my knees, until I could get to my feet without startling her, then went into the house and sat in the dining room, where I could watch her through a window. Five minutes passed. Ten. I thought of George, how sure he was, how capable, making nothing of what he had done. Had the doe tried to bolt as he lifted her out of the water, she might have kicked out, the sharp, deadly hoof slashing into his face, cracking his skull. The minutes passed. My mind began to wander. I looked away from time to time, at the mail, catalogues on the table, looked back, to be sure she was still there. I glanced at the headlines of yesterday's paper, heard George in the kitchen, looked back. I wanted to watch her leave.

But it was too late. This time she was gone.

I got up from the table, walked back outside, to the spot where she had lain. I turned full circle. There was no sign of her, only the sun and the grass and the trees. And my yellow terry cloth robe, on the ground at my feet.

Friday. Even when you know someone is having a heart attack, it can be hard to imagine that he will die. George lay against the raised back of the gurney in the hospital's emergency room. He closed his eyes, opened them again, looked off into the middle distance.

"How are you feeling?" I asked.

"Lousy."

He could have been suffering from the flu.

Earlier that morning, he had come out of the bathroom after his shower, lain back on the bed in his underwear.

"I'm not going anywhere today," he said.

I sat down on the bed, stroked his back.

"You don't feel well?"

"No."

"What's the matter?"

"Pain." He thumped his fist against his chest.

"I'm going to call the doctor."

"I don't want a doctor. My heart's the one thing I can count on. It always comes through on its own."

But he did not protest when, after talking to the doctor, I called for an ambulance.

I started gathering his clothes.

"Where's your flannel shirt? I want you to be warm."

"In the closet in the study."

I found the shirt, but it was dirty, and I returned to his bureau.

"It's in the closet," he insisted.

"I know, but it's dirty. You're going to an emergency room. I want to be sure they treat you with respect."

The paramedics arrived, and the police. George lay on the bed, in white shirt and navy trousers now, black socks.

They administered oxygen, took his blood pressure, his pulse, opened his shirt, attached the sensors of a portable heart monitor to his chest.

"Has there been any shortness of breath?"

"Some."

"Have you ever had a heart attack?"

"A mild one. Years ago."

"Do you take any heart medications now?"

"Nitroglycerin."

"For angina?"

"That's right."

The tall, black policeman asked me for a medical history. The paramedics wrapped George's overcoat around him, lifted him into a stair-chair, pushed him through the apartment, to the hallway and into the elevator, to the lobby and the street, where they transferred him onto a stretcher and into the ambulance.

"What hospital do you usually go to?"

"St. Luke's."

The driver pulled away from the curb, drove, without siren, to the hospital.

"I need some more of that good air," George said, to the paramedic who rode in the back with us. The paramedic checked the gauge on the cylinder of oxygen, then pulled the cylinder from the mask tubing and attached a new one.

In the emergency room, they transferred him to a hospital gurney, wheeled him into a curtained cubicle. Nurses, doctors came and went, huddled around him, checking his pulse, blood pressure, respiration rate, gave him a shot of morphine, hooked up an IV of dextrose and saline, drew blood. I sat on a stool at his side, jumping out of the way as they approached or turned to leave.

One of the residents listened to his heart, lungs, felt the pulse in his neck.

"Tell me what's been happening, Mr. Schieffelin," he said.

Once the EKG had been completed, the doctor led me to the nurses' station.

"Your husband is having a heart attack," he said. I touched my back to the counter of the nurses' station to keep my bearings. "I'm sorry to have to tell you that." He was being so kind to me.

"I suspected as much," I replied, affecting an air of professionalism that would tell him he needn't worry that I would fall apart, make a scene.

In the cardiac unit, the cardiologist asked me to sign a release to allow them to insert a temporary pacemaker.

"We insert the pacemaker wire into the internal jugular and thread it through the superior vena cava into the right ventricle."

I nodded.

"But there are risks to the procedure. There is a chance of puncturing a vein or the wall of the heart, and the pacemaker wire could trigger a rapid, or even life-threatening, arrhythmia. I just want to be sure you understand that."

The cardiologist was an attractive woman in her thirties or early forties, a sound, sympathetic person who talked straight.

"But you think it should be done?"

"Yes, I do. We would also insert what we call a Swan-Ganz catheter to measure the pressure in the pulmonary artery."

I signed the release form, watched from across the hall as they lifted George from the gurney, laid him flat on a shiny, metal table, leaned over, started to work on him, closed the door.

I spent much of the afternoon with Dick's son Dave in the makeshift waiting room at the end of the hall. Someone was always working on George, with an air of busy pre-occupation that told us to stay away. Patients less critically ill walked the halls in robes and slippers, watched television, received visitors. On one venture into George's room, I found him vomiting into a metal dish.

"I guess I came at the wrong time," I said.

"You sure did." He grinned.

Late in the afternoon, Dick arrived from New Haven. George was in a hospital gown, the back of his bed raised. The four lines of the monitor overhead showed his heart rate, blood pressure, the pressure in the pulmonary artery, respiration. The cardiologist came into the room.

"I'd just like to know what I should be doing," George said to her.

"What you should be doing?"

"To get well," he said, with a boyish smile.

"The best thing you can do is to rest, Mr. Schieffelin."

She motioned us into the hallway.

"The echocardiogram looks bad," she said. "I'm afraid there's a fifty to eighty percent chance he won't survive."

But didn't that mean there was a twenty to fifty percent chance that he would?

At ten o'clock, the nurse asked us to leave. I waved to him once more from the doorway of his room, yearning to run back to him. He held my eyes for a moment, waved, looked again into the middle distance. He knew he was alone.

Saturday. Jack had arrived from California. George drifted in and out, sometimes lucid, sometimes confused. He lay in the bed, the back raised, pointing toward a corner of the room.

"There," he said.

"What?" I turned in the direction he was pointing.

"There."

On a shelf above the sink was an aerosol can of Lysol spray, metallic gold, aqua, catching the light.

"What about it?"

He jabbed his finger at it in frustration.

"You want me to move it?"

"Yes."

"He's just projecting his pain, Laurie," Jack said. "It won't help."

I moved it anyway. It didn't help. But at least it told him that I wanted to.

My mind wandered as a television film prompted a rush of stories of his time in the navy. Nurses took his temperature, recorded urinary output, checked IVs.

Disoriented again, he rambled, dozed, grew agitated. I began to sense the presence of some invisible looming force, some malevolent field of energy that was coming to devour me.

Shortly before we left, he roused himself from sleep, opened his eyes, looked at me.

"You and I just know about Stanley Steamers," he pronounced, luxuriating in our shared affinity for steam, this odd attachment that set us apart, united us.

Sunday.

"Don't forget his glasses," Dick called to me.

"I won't."

"You know how frantic he always gets for his glasses and his watch."

I collected his shaving things, his hairbrush, his glasses. He was wearing his watch. For once, the hospital had not insisted that he surrender it.

He was in a coma when we arrived. Flat on his back, the bed lowered, the skin of his face dry, gray. He struggled for breath. I held his glasses, his shaving kit, in my hands. It was clear now that he would die.

I ran from the room, lunged in one direction, then another, desperate for a place to cry. Jack caught up with me.

"Do you need someone to hug?" he said.

I fell into his arms and he held me tight as I sobbed on his gray-suited shoulder.

The day passed. We stood by George's bed, holding his unresponsive hands, as he labored to breathe, drawing in the air, expelling it with a roar that I took to signal his defiance of death, his unwillingness to die.

"You tell 'em, George," I wanted to shout.

My neck, jaw muscles, shoulders were held rigid, as if paralyzed, by that all-engulfing force I had only sensed the day before. Each time I succeeded in pushing my voice through its grip it surprised me. Surprised me too that no one seemed to notice anything strange in me. Every half hour or so, I left for the ladies' room, where I could sit for a few minutes, in tears.

"Only two of us will be allowed to stay after visiting hours," Jack said. "Do you want to stay, Laurie, or would you like to go home and rest?" We stepped back as an orderly wheeled a gurney out of the elevator.

"I'm not leaving until he dies."

"That may be two or three days. You can't stay all that time."

"Well, I'm going to."

Dick and I sat at his side. George's hand lay lightly in mine. The lines on the monitor pulsed their jagged course. His chest lifted as he gasped for air, fell as he expelled it, lifted, fell. Hysteria bubbled in my throat, threatening to erupt in peals of helpless laughter, endless siren screams. Then all was quiet. George lay as if suspended in time, no longer breathing. One second, two seconds, five seconds, ten. . . . The bottom monitor line was flat. Now that I knew it was inevitable, I ached for him to die, for his suffering to be over. With a stentorian inhalation, his chest lifted again. The line pulsed. I thought of what remained of his damaged heart, beating, beating. But it couldn't last, the job was too big, the muscle was tiring, soon it would have to rest.

The night nurse introduced herself, left us alone. I looked at George's hand, the long, strong, beautiful fingers. He was no longer in that hand, but in some distant place, just trying to breathe.

Muffled footsteps passed by in the corridor. I could hear the voices, but not the words, of the hospital personnel, gathered at the nurses' station. Again George stopped breathing.

"Don't start again," I begged silently. "Don't start." Five seconds, ten seconds, fifteen. . . . Then the desperate inhalation.

Dick got out of his chair, sighed softly, walked out into the hallway. I rested my cheek against George's hand, my nose touching the edge of the sheet. My own heart surged with despair. I sat back again. Almost imperceptibly, his hand tensed, the fingers closing, slightly, around mine, then went limp again. His hand had not moved all day. An involuntary reflex, the doctors would say. I think that for a moment he knew I was there. I think it was an act of love.

The nurse returned with a bowl of water and a cloth, sat on the edge of the bed. Putting the bowl on the table, she took a pair of translucent rubber gloves, pulled them over her hands, smoothing the fingers, one by one. She dipped the cloth into the water, then ran it inside George's cheek, along his upper jaw, wetted it again, cleaning, moistening the gums and teeth, dry and scaly with old vomit, the continued struggle for breath. She wetted it yet again, ran it over his lower jaw, his lips. Such a simple act of kindness, surely not required, but one human being respecting the dignity of another, though *in extremis,* still worthy of her care. I could have been in the presence of an angel.

She left the room and Dick returned, sat at George's side. I rounded the foot of the bed, reached for my can of club soda on the table by the door, turned. George lay quiet. No longer breathing. I looked at the lines on the monitor. All four were flat. Flat. Still flat.

"Dick! Go get the doctor to turn off the pacemaker!"

I didn't want it to restart his heart, only to have him have to die again.

The resident on duty raced into the room, looked at the monitor, felt for the pulse in George's neck, listened for a heartbeat, turned off the pacemaker. He checked his watch. 9:43.

"You have my sympathies," he said, before leaving the room.

I traced my fingers over George's brow, the slight dip into his forehead, along one cheekbone, the other, down the curve of his cheek. I ran the flat of my hand over his chest, grazing the sensors, down his arm, along the soft skin beyond the sleeve of his hospital gown. Looked at his beautiful face. Eyes closed, lips parted, head tilted to the side. He was so ineffably sweet.

Dick went about the business of death. I heard him ask about the death certificate, arrangements for removal of the body. He returned, put on his hat and coat, waited for me.

I couldn't stop touching George's face, his body. I kissed his forehead, leaving an imprint of All Day Mocha Pink.

"Do you want to take his watch?" Dick asked.

"No, leave it. He always felt unmanned without his watch."

The resident burst into the room again, surprised to find us still there.

"My sympathies," he spluttered, before leaving again.

No doubt another patient was waiting for the bed. But this was the person I had loved more than anything in my life.

I stood at his side, kissed him again. Caressed the soft growth of beard.

"He always loved the idea of Lucy Mercer's being with FDR when he died," I said to Dick.

"I know."

"He would say so pointedly, 'He died in her arms.' "

"I know."

"I wish he had died in my arms."

"I think he did."

Dick went into the hallway again and I stood, drinking George in with my eyes, touching his brow, his cheek, the thick white hair. He lay, so utterly still. When I left the room, he would be gone.

I leaned down to kiss him again. His forehead was cool. I stood up. It was over now. It was time to go home.

After the service in New York, we gathered at the grave site at the tiny country cemetery in New Jersey, Jack and Dick, their families, George's English cousins, my brother, Lewis and his wife, three close woman friends. The day was crystalline. The heavy wet snow of the day before sparkled in the soft, warm sun, billowed along the branches of the trees. I held the simple walnut box, containing George's ashes, at my waist.

The young curate who had accompanied us stood in cassock, surplice, and stole, faced us across the grave, read from his prayer book, which lay flat in his lifted hand.

"O God, whose mercies cannot be numbered; Accept our prayers on behalf of the soul of thy servant departed, and grant him an entrance into the land of light and joy, . . ."

I felt a thunk on the back of my head, the cold dust of snow on my neck. Another chunk grazed the blond head of the curate, landed with a plop on his open prayer book. Startled, he was silent for a moment, then dusted off his book and continued, ". . . in the fellowship of thy saints; through Jesus Christ our Lord. Amen."

I smiled. The air swelled with our collective delight. Here was George, irrepressible as always, telling us not to be so solemn, cackling, at this ultimate cosmic joke, as he threw snow at us from the trees.

My kitchen window frames a palette of autumn—the holly berries, now russet orange, echoing the reddish gold of the glimpse of maple just visible behind the long-needled pines. The pine needles themselves turning gold. And all of it anchored in the foreground by the rich burgundy of the dogwood.

The computer installer arrives to hook up my new computer. He blusters in, exclaiming over the backup on Route 287, how late he is.

"Could I use your phone?" he asks. "I have one more customer after I finish here, but I'll just have to blow him off."

Blow him off! Here he is in his coat and tie telling me he's going to blow somebody off! It must be just an everyday expression! Still, it's one I don't think I'll try to use.

I open one of the overhead doors of the garage and out bursts Mrs. Danforth's black-and-white kitten. He has been trapped for at least a couple of days, as I haven't gone into the garage since Tuesday. I gather him up and carry him to his front door.

"There you are!" Mrs. Danforth cries. "Where have you been?"

She takes him from me and scratches him under the chin, then puts him on the ground at her feet. He marches into a patch of pachysandra to pee.

"Uh, oh," I say to Mrs. Danforth, with what I fear may be a half-hearted smile. "I wonder how he's been handling that for the past two days."

I search the inside of the garage, imagining unwanted pools and other deposits on the hoods, the upholstered leather seats of the antique cars. But I find nothing. Until I look at the floor under the rear of the Stanley, where the handfuls of Kitty Litter, which I have tossed under the engine to catch dripping steam cylinder oil, have been carefully gathered into a conscientious, stool-filled little pile.

I merely open the door to the cellar and Murray bounds into the dining room, whips past me through the door, he-man shoulders rippling as he clumps down the narrow wooden stairs. Mariah, more cautious, sniffs at the doorsill as I follow Murray, garbage bags and flashlight in hand. The beam of my flashlight catches the sump pump at the foot of the stairs, the old screens and storm windows leaning against the foundation wall. I turn, and, ducking my head, make my way between the maroon-colored Lally columns, to the back wall, and the furnace, the hot water heater, the water pump, their myriad angles of pipe. The concrete floor, dry now that the downspouts have been extended, the cistern closed off, is coated with a grainy film of red New Jersey soil, washed in during innumerable earlier rains. I tighten the bulb in the socket overhead. At my feet are the piles of old burlap that I have decided I cannot tolerate for another day.

"You know all that burlap in the corner by the water pump?" I had asked Lewis.

"I remember."

"Do you think I could get rid of it?"

"Oh, sure. You don't need that."

"What was it for?"

"Mr. Schieffelin used to have me wrap the pipes with it

in winter, and stuff it into the opening to the crawl space. So
the pipes wouldn't freeze. But he had the outside of the
crawl space closed off a few years ago. And the furnace is
right there."

I put my flashlight on the floor by the furnace and shake
open the first of my brown Hefty bags, reach for the nearest
hunk of burlap. It is crusty, gray, and it holds its shape as I
peel it from the floor. Dirt and dust rain down from it, along
with the corpses of insects of various types, all with many
legs. A cloud of dust blows into my face as I push the burlap
into my bag. Murray rolls happily amid a row of rusty coffee
cans, sections of copper tubing, electric wire, and several
white marbles.

Who would have thought, three months ago, that I
would ever putter around my cellar with such equanimity?
Not only that. Come to think of it, I've even managed not to
worry about the lightning.

I stuff the bags of burlap into my garbage cans. It is a
brisk October day. A tank truck delivers fuel oil to the
house next door. Before me is the new storm window
Wayne has made for the kitchen window, the new gutter
along the flat roof of the kitchen, and above, the white
aluminum trim along the edge of the upper roof. So much
work done. The hedge, forsythia, holly tree are trimmed to
manageable size, and grass grows thick where the fountain
used to be. Along the side of the house, the honeysuckle is

gone, the boxwood shaped, the branches of wisteria woven inward. The new porch posts are bold with new paint, the casing crisp around the windows and the new storm/screen doors. I continue around the house, past extended downspouts, the foundation, newly pointed up, the bank of topsoil that covers the filled-in cistern, the new section of septic drain. New grass covers the topsoil, the ditch and the holes that Ed has filled in.

I think of the men who have helped me—Bob Beck, Wayne, Paul, Mike Kravik, Ed, the others. It is they and those like them who form the backbone of a nation. We forget how we depend on them, the unvaunted skill of good, honest work.

It is a similar honesty, I think, that is part of the appeal of my house. My house makes no claims, has no pretensions, is simply a house, grown worn with the passage of time. But it is a home. There is a nobility in its simplicity. And now that it has been repaired, I am secure in its embrace.

It is still a bit of an eyesore. The asbestos shingles, the blocks of the porch rail, are still gray for lack of paint. New weeds will push through the cracks in the concrete walks. Other window casings will have to be replaced. Everyone urges me to get rid of the asbestos shingles, install new vinyl siding. That means I'll have to find licensed white-suited men, with masks, who will come for a maximum of four hours a day, to remove and dispose of the asbestos.

But I am battened down for winter now. I'll think about that in the spring.

Another NOTICE about the road!

"Our own township traffic consultant thinks we should have an *immediate* four-lane county road, and in some areas would like to put up cement barriers in the center. We'll be living on a major throughway.

"We all need to wake up and take a vital part in this matter * Write to your township committee * Write to your freeholders * Attend the township committee meetings (1st and 3rd Mondays of each month, 7:30 P.M.)."

After talking to the woman in the deli, I had decided not to think about the road. But maybe I'd better wake up. Go to the township meeting. At least I'd find out who the players are.

I once said to George, "I'd be lost without you."

"On the contrary," he replied, "I hope I'll have taught you how to live."

He is a good model. In his affection for people, his refusal to take (most) things too seriously, his jubilant pursuit of his dreams.

I have learned too, from losing him. Grief is such a

mixture of elements—pain, guilt, anger, terror, helpless-
ness. I realize now that my fears about the house grew out of
my feeling that I had lost control of my destiny. That if your
husband can die, anything can happen to you. The process of
grief is so full of contradictions—writhing with the pain,
and cherishing it because it means he is still there. Losing
one's sense of place in the everyday world, but becoming part
of a larger natural cycle, achieving a new sense of place, not
contingent on earthly rewards or the reward of a Heaven.
Losing, at least for a time, the fear of death, and seeing, does
one dare say it?, its beauty. In the agony of grief, there are
moments of peace. And, always, the joy of love recalled.

Grief teaches us what is important. It makes the joys
more joyous, the sorrows more acute—not only one's own
but those of others. And so one grows in empathy, and in
compassion. Through grief one experiences life at its most
intense. And if one does not live intensely, perhaps one does
not live at all.

George will be the touchstone of the rest of my life. I
will try to live in a way that would please him, will keep him
with me by doing so. Until his death, I had been content to
remain in his shadow. But I'm on my own now. It is up to
me to make of my life what I can. He has taught me how
important it is to meet life head-on. And how important it
is to seize your dreams.

I open the small chest of drawers in the living room, pull
out a short paragraph I wrote for the rector to read at
George's funeral. I remember writing it, at the small kitchen

table in the apartment, tears pouring down my face. It was meant to sum up who he was. And it was my goodbye.

I sit down on the sofa to read it again.

"As we who loved him know best, George Schieffelin was no ordinary man. He touched the lives of all of us with his kindness, his generosity of spirit, and his delight. As the gleam grew in his eye, the most mundane details of daily life grew endlessly entertaining; calamity became a delicious joke. An obstacle, for him, was simply incentive. His gleeful outrageousness was simply disarming. He was a man of honor, compassionate and wise, who knew that life was to be lived—and live it he did. A light has gone out of *our* lives and we will miss him."

I get up from the sofa and return the paragraph to the drawer. It is Monday. 7:25 in the evening. I take my jacket from the chair in the dining room, the car keys from the table, and walk out the door and down the steps to the driveway. It is time to go and see what I can do about that road.